...ATS AND

WEALTH

...and Lies of the
...ement Industry

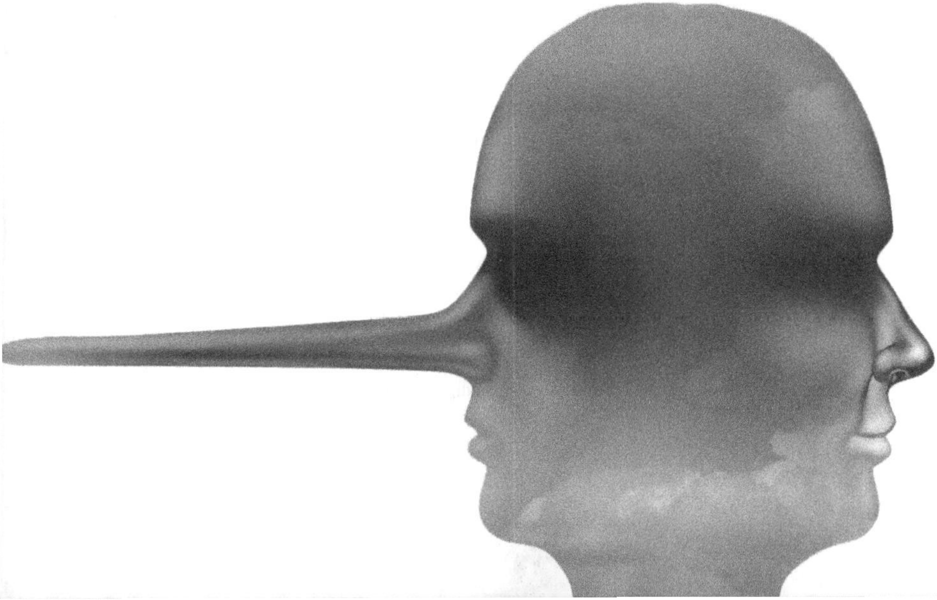

Editorial Project Management: Karen Rowe, karenrowe.com
Cover Design: Angela Hammersmith, hammersmithgraphics.com
Interior Layout: Ljiljana Pavkov, bookwormsdesign.com

Printed in the United States.

ISBN: 979-8-9913635-0-1 (paperback)
ISBN: 979-8-9913635-1-8 (digital)

To all the business owners who inspired this book:
you are the risk-takers who provide the jobs,
healthcare, stability, and sustainability the U.S.
so desperately needs.

In matters of style,
swim with the current;
in matters of principle,
stand like a rock.

—TRADITIONAL ADAGE

CONTENTS

DEAD CATS AND WEALTH ADVISORS

INTRODUCTION

Paul*, a business owner in Florida in his fifties, has $10 million already invested with a discount brokerage because his father taught him to hate financial advisors. His father has a financial personality type that my firm refers to as an Accumulator, meaning he's very frugal.

Paul gets referred to us by an attorney who has been a client as well as a member of our advisory team for twenty years. Paul has built a roofing company, and we spend a hundred man-hours helping him with the

---

*Examples and stories are used for illustrative purposes only and should not be deemed a representation of past or future results. They do not represent any specific product, nor do they reflect sales charges or other expenses. They do not represent specific advice.

business exit. We get him a 31 percent increase in return for the business by bringing in our team. We do a ton of planning. We get a tax plan ready, a charitable plan ready, and an income plan for after his company is sold. He works with our lifetime transition counselor, at no additional cost.

We take over management of half the money from the discount broker. In the last year, our returns have performed better with less volatility. Because we're ethical, we tell him to keep $3 million in the bank of the $27 million that he sells the business for. It provides him stability, since he's newly retired and there's been a big life change. We also set aside some of the reserve fund to pay the tax bill that's coming the following year. We don't charge any fee on that $3 million, because it's the right thing to do.

THE POUNCE

We advise Paul to go to his bank and at least make sure it's giving him a competitive return on those deposits. We could get him 5 percent, but we want him to have it at the bank he's comfortable dealing with. As long as the interest rate is reasonable, there is no need to disrupt his life further.

He calls the bank just to inquire about CD rates, but then *bam!* The pounce happens. All of a sudden, the bank's wealth management guys call him, saying, "Hey, we know you work with a different wealth management firm, but you really ought to talk to our wealth management team."

This is why my industry sucks. They waited until the assets were there to manage, and *then* they pounced. This behavior infuriates me. Where were these lazy opportunists when he needed help a year ago? Where were they when he was afraid and didn't even know if he could afford to sell his business, retire, and sustain his lifestyle? Imagine if your doctor refused to treat you for a common illness or minor procedure *but* came alive the minute you needed heart surgery, owing to the fact that heart surgery is where the big money is. This is quite similar to my industry, where advisors "pounce" on you for the opportunity to make money only after you have a big liquidity event. Despicable! I'm writing this book because I hate the pounce. You deserve clear-eyed guidance through your most difficult financial decisions, and the wealth management advice you receive should serve *you*, not an opportunist's sales commission.

THE TROUBLING TRUTH

You might not want to hear it, but there are two main problems getting in the way of properly managing your wealth.

It's You

You are one of those problems. As a society, we seem to have forgotten or lost the concept of personal responsibility. However you came to have your wealth—whether you built and sold a business quickly, spent forty years growing assets, or inherited your money—it demands a great amount of personal responsibility. Yes, from *you* to make good decisions about what you do with it.

How do you coordinate it? How do you manage it? You can use it for many things: for the greater good, for charity, for generational stability. You can use it for your children. You can use it to pay for healthcare. Ultimately it is your choice, your burden, and your responsibility. It can also be your greatest joy. Yet one of the biggest problems facing many ultra-high-net-worth families is getting past their own fear and inertia. Inertia is insidious. Doing nothing when you know you should act means losing money in a gradual, subtle way—with harmful effects.

Have you ever heard of a wealth stress test? Has your advisor ever performed one for your family? How often does your team—including your CPA, estate attorney, financial advisor, and insurance agent—meet in a coordinated fashion to work on nothing but your concerns? Do your advisors know you and your family at a genuine human level, including your weaknesses, values, and deeply held beliefs? These are just a few key questions that you should be asking when assessing your financial advisor. But many investors are complacent and comfortable with the status quo, even when they know that their current advisor doesn't serve their best interests.

It's Your Financial Advisor

The other problem is your financial advisor: chances are, they may not have your best interests at heart. As I have observed my industry for the last thirty-six years by listening at conferences, mastermind groups, and educational forums, the people taking care of your money all claim to be wealth managers—but in my experience, most "advisors" can be product pushers with an agenda to sell specific products. More painfully, they have duped the public into accepting less than they deserve. When my wife, Sonya, came into the industry in 2011 and began attending conferences and educational sessions, she disliked the male-centric event and said, "There is a reason for the term 'finance bros.'" The advisors we met often came across as self-serving, braggadocious, and egotistical. They didn't ask any questions or try to engage in actual conversation. Instead, they talked *at* us about themselves and their great business model.

Early in my career, I was one of the top salespeople at a well-known investment and insurance company. The company sponsored a sales contest in which the top three salespeople won a trip to Pebble Beach, California, where we would meet Johnny Miller, who was the best golfer in the world at the time. He had come to have dinner and golf with us.

In my youthful naivety, I did not realize that this contest may have created a conflict of interest. It encouraged me to sell products to clients that they might not have needed. I sure as hell was not there because I had made a positive impact on the client's lives. The reward was strictly promotional for selling the products of the big company where I worked.

I now realize what a corrupt business model this was: pretending to be an estate and financial advisor, when in fact, I was nothing more than a product peddler.

Later in my career, in the early 2000s, my partners and I worked with a firm that decided to change the company we were affiliated with, so we moved to a different brokerage firm that was a subsidiary of a life insurance company. We were on the company's sales rewards cruise for being some of its top brokers. (Once again, we were being rewarded for selling products instead of focusing on the best ways to help families.)

The CEO of the new company was on that ship. He made a very blunt announcement, speaking to the hundreds and hundreds of financial advisors who were in the room. He said, point-blank, that in order to remain part of that advisory firm going forward, we would have to be willing to sell his company's products, its annuities, and whatever funds it might offer.

This arrangement is the equivalent of a doctor who is also a salesperson for a drug company or a medical device company. What are the chances that they will lead with holistic advice—such as diet and exercise—or offer other available treatments, solutions, surgeries, or pharmaceutical alternatives? Even if a pharmaceutical is a necessary intervention, will they suggest the competition's offerings or start by recommending their own company's drug option? Such a situation incentivizes professionals to put their own interests and the interests of their employer above those of the client. It becomes a question of ethics.

At least our new CEO was honest and up-front on that cruise: in effect, we were now the drug dealer, not the advisor. He did not try to hide that we were effectively just part of that company's distribution model. We would have to push its products over others that might have been more suitable for a client.

I understand why wealthy families often hire huge banks, major brokerages, and generally large, well-known firms for their wealth management: familiar branding creates a perception of safety. But bigger is not always better, and the misconception is based in ignorance—investors don't know or don't want to know the difference. As long as it's working fairly well, why would they move?

And what's worse, you probably already know the big commission-based firms aren't serving you. The gap between the needs and desires of wealthy families and the services provided by their advisors is astounding and currently at an all-time high. There has been a significant increase in the dissatisfaction of high-net-worth individuals with their wealth advisors. Based on Spectrem Group research, 22 percent of high-net-worth-families are looking to fire their advisor.[1] In some ways, this is a very good sign because it means consumers are waking up to the shortcomings of the wealth management industry—but the information is only helpful if you are willing to do something about it.

Our research indicates there is a yawning gap in the industry between what clients need and what advisors deliver. The heat map below summarizes the main shortcomings, illustrating the discrepancy between the desires of wealthy investors, the promises the industry makes, and the services they actually receive.

---

[1] Spectrem Group, Wealth Spectrem: Wealth Management Redefined. 2022.

Wealthy Investor Services Heat Map

	Investment Management	Tax Planning	Estate Planning	Wealth Protection Planning	Charitable Planning
Services desired by wealthy investors	92.1%	89.2%	91.1%	73.8%	87.3%
Services received by wealthy investors from their advisors	72.1%	24.8%	22.4%	7.5%	6.0%

N = 416 investors, 706 advisors

©2023 CEG Insights

For instance, 91.1 percent of wealthy investors desired estate planning advice, but only 22.4 percent received it. While 73.8 percent of wealthy investors reported wanting wealth protection planning, only 7.5 percent reported having advisors who offered this service. And 87.3 percent of wealthy investors said that charitable planning was important to them; yet only 6 percent of advisors provided this service.

These numbers bear out that families are no longer accepting the status quo. They are demanding more from the industry. People gravitate to the big financial institutions because of the perceived safety. The good news is that once you understand that big investment and financial institutions are not your friend—that they actually exist to grow and protect themselves—you can make better choices.

The financial services industry was born to make itself money. It's too easy for ultra-high-net-worth families like yours to slip through the cracks, not get your needs met, or find out too late that your broker is not a wealth planner or fiduciary. These are reasons why the industry fails you and why I'm writing this book.

Having great wealth creates complex problems that are too great to manage yourself, and until and unless clients demand more from their financial advisors, the neglect will continue.

SOLIDIFYING YOUR FAMILY'S LEGACY

There's a better way. I believe deeply in merit, personal accountability, personal responsibility, and equal opportunity for all. The importance of generational stability and responsibility cannot be overstated. I am driven to educate heirs and instill values to ensure smooth transitions of wealth and prevent family discord. An integrated team of experts working together on your wealth can help cement your legacy.

Having observed the worst practices in financial advising, I realized the best way to hold the industry accountable was to build a business that was better than anything ultra-high-net-worth clients could obtain from traditional brokerage and wealth management firms. Thus, my own purpose has become clear: disrupt the industry by modeling perfection and setting the gold standard. The solution is a comprehensive, coordinated wealth management process that helps wealthy families break out of complacency and inertia to reimagine what's possible with their resources—whether that's lifestyle, philanthropy, or legacy planning. My true mission is to build my own comprehensive wealth practice, which I call a virtual family office (or VFO, more on that in Chapter 3), and disrupt the entire industry by alarming and arming the public with the knowledge to make more informed choices about their wealth management.

This book will empower and educate wealthy families and hardworking business owners to find the right financial advisor and wealth management services to truly optimize their hard-earned wealth and solidify their legacy for generations. You will learn to identify and avoid the "Circle of Vultures"—advisors and professionals who may have conflicts of interest or may not be acting in their clients' best interests. I'll outline the different tiers of financial advice, from brokers to true wealth managers, and provide a framework for evaluating potential advisors. You will discover the power of a VFO approach to coordinating all your financial and legal affairs, as well as strategies for amplifying generational stability and avoiding common mistakes.

By the end, my hope is that you will have the knowledge and tools to take control of your wealth and help ensure it is managed effectively to fulfill your goals and represent your highest values for many generations to come.

SCREAM IT FROM THE MOUNTAINTOP

I can't help but get on my soapbox and scream from the mountaintop: I've concluded my industry is largely a bunch of posers. If you attend conferences and collectives where financial advisors or wealth managers gather, they do a lot of posturing. Just listening to their words, you would think that they truly understood the soul of each and every client. When you look under the hood, though, it is a bunch of bull spit.

THE CIRCLE OF VULTURES

As an ultra-high-net-worth individual, you have a target on your back. As your wealth and visibility grow, so does that target. If you are in this category and have dozens or maybe even hundreds of employees, you are one of the United States' most productive citizens. You create the jobs, the healthcare, and the stability that the country so desperately needs. Without you, there is no sustainability. You also deserve to be defended and protected from this "Circle of Vultures."

Sadly, the vultures can come from outside the fort or inside the fort. In other words, they can be people you already know and probably trust—your golf buddy, a sibling, an old friend, or anyone else who has a seat at your table. The vultures outside the fort often come from the financial advice or insurance industries. Trust me: I know, as I started my career over thirty years ago as a life insurance agent and investment broker. My main intention then was to make myself money. As I learned about the predatory practices of this industry, I fought hard to develop a customer-centric solution that didn't present a conflict of interest.

Do you feel like your advisory team is defending you and your interests? Are the members of your team coordinating and meeting on a regular basis? If not, they probably cannot know and protect your interests. Has your team ever performed, or much less even heard of, a wealth stress test? If not, maybe the vultures are circling overhead.

EXPOSING INDUSTRY FLAWS

Ethical practitioners must loudly spread the word about how the financial advice industry really works. I feel very strongly about this issue as a thirty-six-year industry veteran. I began my career by having to sell my employer's products exclusively while claiming that I was an "advisor." The big challenge in our industry is that anyone (and I mean virtually *anyone*) can call themselves a financial advisor, even without a securities license. Some advisors only have a license to sell life insurance and certain types of fixed annuities.

People can call themselves financial advisors even when they are not capable, competent, or qualified. Yet it is evident to me that many Americans—even ultra-high-net-worth Americans—often don't understand that simple reality, because of the factors I'll explain below.

This situation leads to many wealthy business owners feeling ignored, taken for granted, and outright exploited by the financial advice industry. Sadly, I have found that most of the advice industry overcharges for fees or commissions, while often ignoring the client completely. I am regularly dismayed when I hear from a new client or even a wealthy friend that they must reach out to their financial advisor if they want meetings or counsel, sometimes needing to call ten times to get an appointment. I just listen and shake my head. It has become something of a mission for me to expose these problematic dynamics within the wealth management and financial advice industry.

Another common issue is that the *client*—the one paying for the financial advice—often feels "talked down to." I believe that the advisors who use this tactic do so because they think they can only keep their jobs if the client feels that the subject is over their head— too complex and too difficult to understand. From that place of ignorance, clients may feel that they must hire an advisor and pay their fee unquestioningly. However, cultivating that power dynamic reflects deep insecurity on the part of the financial advisor.

IT'S THE PLANNING, STUPID

I'm likely going to be the only one in my industry who says things to you like "It's the planning, stupid" or "Don't be a dunce." I want to be clear that this is not a personal attack, but if someone isn't that direct, you'll never change. I've concluded that I'm okay with being a little bit coarse, because everyone is trying to be kind and politically correct, but they're not really helping you.

Portfolio management has become table stakes in my world. In the old days, advisors could differentiate themselves by saying, "My fund is better than their fund." With technology, increased awareness, and the advent of companies like Vanguard and Charles Schwab, clients can now manage portfolios for free on their own.

So advisors had to find new ways to add value. To illustrate this point, allow me to share a quick story*. There's a business owner in his midforties who is married with two young children. He sells his business for $70 million. He gets an initial payment, with future payments depending on company performance. He takes that first $30 million and gives it to a local advisor with one of those huge institutions that I love so much.

A year after the sale, he's confused. He doesn't understand the legal documents he signed relating to the sale. A family member tells him to meet with my firm because he wants a yacht and a private island. Well, guess what? He's not that rich. Yes, it's a lot of money, but it's not "private island money." We have lunch with the family and discover they have no estate plan.

It's the planning, stupid!

He's paying $100,000 a year to an advisor at the big institution to manage his money, but it's clear that advisor is lazy and doesn't care about his family, period. This family deserves more. They deserve better.

I keep coming back to this: wealth is just a tool to optimize people's lives. Sitting quietly became a non-option for me, so I built an exceptional solution that would optimize the client's life rather than enriching the financial advisor and the big companies they worked for.

As I confess frequently, I used to be one of the bad guys. My first seven years in the industry, I was a selfish product salesman. Truth is, I was hungry for more money, and everyone who had some looked like a big juicy steak to me.

Just like my misguided youth hanging out with the wrong crowd, I slowly grew out of this and began raising my standards, though it was a decades-long journey for which I am still happily paying my penance today.

This process led to the birth of the virtual family office business, and finally—almost begrudgingly—my quest to vocally hold the industry accountable.

I hope to have thousands of haters after this book comes out.

THE HIERARCHY OF FINANCIAL ADVICE

When I first started in the financial services industry, I was grateful that a company would take a risk on hiring me, but I had virtually no network. If you have no clients, you are essentially worthless to an established firm. I was given a form titled "Project One Hundred." The company needed to know that, as a de facto salesperson or broker, I had a network of at least one hundred people I could call to sell to. Can you say Yellow Pages? How silly is it that I was able to get my first job as a life insurance broker by pretending that I knew a hundred people and was willing to call on them? The barrier to entry was so low.

Let's take a closer look at the vultures in the financial advice industry and a tool I refer to as the hierarchy of financial advice. Consumers, particularly wealthy consumers, must know that there are four categories of financial advisors. I use that term loosely because the bottom tier technically, legally, and ethically does not qualify as giving advice. I like to refer to this as the "Four D's": Disappoint, Deliver, Defend, and Defend and Delight.

{Insert Graphic 2: Hierarchy of Financial Advice}

Tier 1: Agent or Broker

A broker or sales agent works on commission, often has sales quotas, and often only represents the products of one company. There is no problem with this arrangement if it is fully disclosed and transparent to the buyer, but all too often it is not. The broker may claim to be a wealth manager or financial advisor, but the experience is very transactional. They're just looking to sell you something. They may not have the client's best interest at heart. I believe there's an inherent conflict of interest.

Disappoint: I define this tier as a disappointment because the "advisor" will sell you something that you may not need or need often. The product is likely to

Hierarchy of Financial Advice

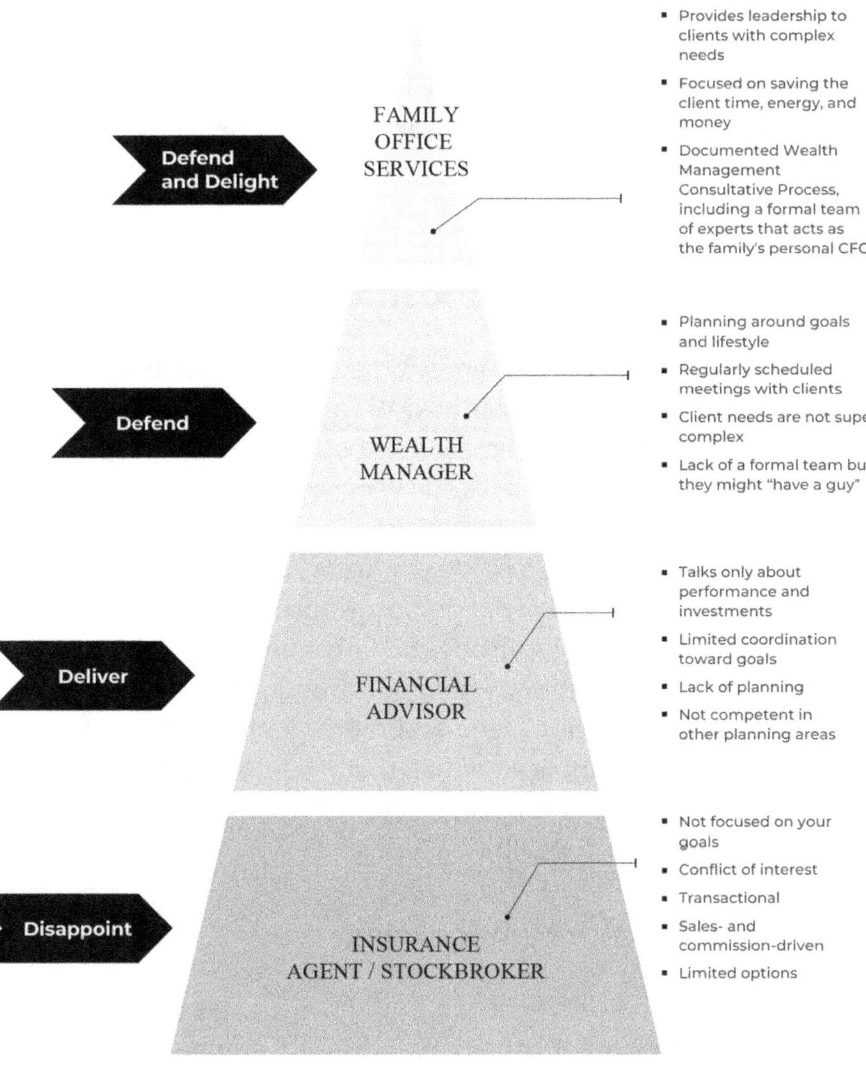

underperform your expectations or goals. Because these brokers are focused more on the transaction, this tier has less emphasis on the best interests of the client. There are times when transactional relationships make sense and are necessary. Paying for your groceries at a cash register is one such example, but the purpose of the transaction is exchanging money for something else. This kind of relationship tends to operate a lot like working with a realtor; they move on once the transaction is complete. There's really no incentive for an insurance agent or a broker to stick around.

Tier 2: Financial or Investment Advisor

At this level, the focus tends to be on investments and performance goals. These advisors are often not competent in other planning areas. They begin to do some rudimentary planning, but it's still very limited and tends to focus only on investments and investment performance. The advice may even be on a fiduciary basis, but these advisors are probably not doing advanced planning.

Deliver: At this level, advisors are starting to deliver. They might be able to help you budget or do some basic planning for college and retirement savings, but it's not more complicated than that. This tier of advice is certainly not for the business owner who has complex needs and more wealth.

Tier 3: Wealth Management

When advisors deliver genuine wealth management, they do the investment consulting, portfolio management, advanced planning, and relationship management.

Advanced planning is much more complicated, as it includes considerations such as tax mitigation, asset protection, charitable planning, and ensuring money reaches heirs in an efficient manner.

Relationship management is the complicated part for wealthy people, who often have multiple advisors, such as a CPA, a tax advisor, an insurance agent, an attorney, and other financial professionals. Wealth managers take responsibility for coordinating all of these team members.

Defend: Defense is key here, as ultra-high-net-worth individuals need protection from insurance agents or attorneys who may want to sell them products or trusts that they don't need.

Tier 4: High-Level Wealth Manager or Family Office Services

The top tier of the hierarchy of financial advice is the "family office," which can include single-family, multifamily, and virtual family offices. The single-family office is typically for individuals with a net worth of $250 million or more. Think Jeff Bezos, Warren Buffet, and Michael Jordan. They have big, complex wealth management needs and create their own family office, a legal entity that exists to off-load the complexities and responsibilities of large wealth. This is a separate corporation or partnership, and the advisors on that payroll only work for one family.

For lower levels of wealth, there is a multifamily office, and in some cases, a virtual family office. I like to say virtual family offices are best for wealthy people who are mere mortals. These tend to be the most productive citizens in the country. They generate the most payroll taxes, meaning they create the most jobs. They tend to be business owners and entrepreneurs who are not wealthy enough to need a single-family office but would still benefit from outsourcing their wealth management.

Defend and Delight: This tier delivers genuine wealth management.

At this level, families frequently need defending from inside and outside the fort. We have seen the many forms this defense can take, such as for our client who owns several manufacturing companies (with a net worth of over $100 million) but has very little liquidity, less than $3 million. During the COVID-19 lockdown, his best golf buddy suggested he invest in a real estate deal he had going. When our VFO real estate expert examined the deal, it turned out to be an operating marina that would have required a $1 million investment, which would remain illiquid for years. It also was in the bottom 25 percent of all operating marinas in the country for profitability. It sucks when we have to defend our clients from a close friend.

Another client in their midfifties hired us to help exit their business. The older partner was in his mid-seventies. We represented the younger partner, who had $50 million after they sold the business. Their best friend worked for a group who began trying to sell them a $10 million life insurance policy under the guise of paying estate taxes. This would have incurred an $80,000 annual premium and an $80,000 commission to the broker.

We conducted a wealth stress test for this client and discovered that they had already been sold $9 million of life insurance. So, if we simply took the existing life insurance and placed it inside an irrevocable life insurance trust, that would get it out of their estate and cover the estate tax. They could save $80,000 a year. In this case, our advice helped them prevent a costly mistake.

IDENTIFY YOUR TYPE

Look at the hierarchy of financial advice and identify which type of advisor you are currently working with.

1. Are they commission-based?
2. Are their products proprietary?
3. More importantly, whom *should* you be working with?

BIGGEST PROBLEMS IN THE INDUSTRY

If you were to look at the marketing materials of all the wealth and financial advisors in the country, you might think the industry understands its clients better than any other, but nothing could be further from the truth.

I know this firsthand because I have interviewed a multitude of wealthy families. According to our in-house research, more than 70 percent of wealthy families are dissatisfied with one or more of their current advisors. They say that they've outgrown their CPAs or their attorneys, and the majority of them are not receiving the high-end advanced planning services that the financial advisory world claims to be delivering.

In this section, I will pull back the curtain on some of the most troubling practices plaguing the wealth management landscape and provide a road map for how investors can protect themselves.

Conflicts of Interest

Looking at a financial advisor's business card has become a litmus test. I can tell in a matter of seconds if they have ulterior motives, limitations, or potential conflicts of interest based solely on that little piece of paper. If an advisor's card lists the name of a company owned by a large life insurance company, I know right away that they don't have all the tools available to best serve their clients.

One of the biggest problems in our industry is most advisors in this country are wolves in sheep's clothing, pretending to represent your family while in fact representing their employers. They are employed by full-service broker-dealers, large insurance companies, and investment firms. I'm sure I don't need to name the "Big Four"—you probably already know the largest full-service firms today. As of 2022, the Big Four employed 15.1 percent of advisors and had 34.1 percent of asset market share.[2]

There are also thousands of smaller competitors described as independent broker-dealers, wealth management advisors, or just plain brokerages, even though

---

[2] Andrew Welsch, "Indie Advisors Outnumber Wirehouse Advisors, but Continue to Lag in Assets," *Barron's*, Oct. 30, 2023, https://www.barrons.com/advisor/articles/ria-wirehouse-advisor-cerulli-associates-64446bd7.

they are not truly "independent."[3] There's a severe conflict of influence since the advisor must sell you, the customer, a certain amount of the insurance company's own product. What are the odds on any given day that a single company has the best and lowest-cost products out of thousands, even millions, of options?

Beyond that, they may be able to charge you "fees" to manage money, an annuity, life insurance, disability insurance, or 529 plans. At the end of the day, their loyalty is to the company and their priority is to push its products.

The question you need to ask of any advisor is: How are they getting paid? But first, you need to understand the fee structure for yourself.

FEE VS. KICKBACK

If I charge you a fee, it creates a direct relationship. You agree to pay me a certain fee. That's coming to me directly. That's not, in fact, a kickback for the financial service company. It's not a commission. It is different: it's a fee for service.

You could pay a retainer fee to design a plan for an eventual business exit, which has nothing to do with your portfolio. That is a case where an advisor is truly acting in a fiduciary capacity.

Some of the bigger investment banks and financial services companies may charge you that fee, but to return to the doctor analogy, they're not looking at the

---

[3] Melanie Waddell, "What the Broker-Dealer Industry Looks Like Now, in 5 Charts," *ThinkAdvisor*, May 5, 2023, https://www. thinkadvisor.com/2023/05/05/what-the-broker-dealer-industry-looks-like-now-in-5-charts-2.

entire universe of drugs; they're selling their own drug. What if one company pays a 6 percent commission and another pays 1 percent, but the one with the lower commission has the better fund? If your advisor is getting paid a commission, there may be an immediate conflict of interest.

BROKER-DEALER BETRAYAL

Another conflict of interest that exists is when a company acts as a broker and a dealer, meaning they are buying and selling on their own behalf. For example, we have seen instances where an advisor put a client in some corporate bonds without going to the market to obtain the best pricing. They simply sold the bonds out of the existing inventory of their brokerage firm.

Advisors like myself who deeply and strongly want to represent the client, not an insurance company or a fund company, must form our own independent firms. Do we occasionally sell insurance because a client needs it? Yes, of course. If I have to send them elsewhere, it requires really trusting someone and dilutes our role.

Recently, a client* needed a $30 million policy to cover his multiple business partners. If he dies, they need the cash to buy out his wife, and they don't have enough on hand. My firm acted as a broker and reviewed three hundred options to find the cheapest policy issued by a strong company. We'll collect a commission on that, but it's rare for us to recommend and broker insurance policies. In this case, it was in the client's best interests. He already trusts us, and his attorney and CPA were the ones to recommend this protection. Our job was to dispense it, and we disclosed the commission to him.

Double-Dipping

The second question you need to ask of an advisor is: Are they truly acting as a fiduciary when giving investment advice? What are you getting for that fee?

Another issue we routinely observe is that investors simply don't know what fees and costs they are already incurring. Imagine that you just bought a new car, and you're hanging out with your buddy when you realize he bought the same car...for $25,000 less. It's essential to understand what you're getting for what you're paying.

We were recently consulting with a family office with a net worth over $300 million, $50 million of which was in liquid portfolios managed by a big, bad institution. Through a deep analysis, we discovered that the fees were very competitive. However, the money was being managed exclusively by the big institution, using only their money managers and in-house funds. They were double-dipping by self-dealing and keeping more of the fees. What I believe to be a true fiduciary process would not be self-serving.

By comparison, our process includes an analysis of approximately twenty thousand institutional money managers, identifying the top one hundred or so in each category. For example, we look at small-cap growth stocks versus foreign stocks versus real estate trusts and only utilize the top performers in each category. We identify the top performers by length of experience in that specialty, proven process, and finally, performance. Since big institutional advisors don't have to do this work, many don't bother, which is sheer laziness.

In our case, we keep each of these money managers on thirty-day rolling contracts so that we can fire them if any of those metrics change.

A family who has spent many decades employing hundreds of people, funding healthcare, and paying a lot of taxes—property and otherwise—deserves better than to pay an institution to self-deal. In my opinion, they deserve someone who truly defends them and has an ongoing process in place to maintain that promise. Understanding who you're working with in the advice space is essential.

Laziness

Another problem in the industry is agents who are only interested in getting to manage your money. The industry call this "assets under management," which can provide a lifelong income to the advisor. We call that focus "yield to broker," not "yield to client," and it's selfish. Such brokers are uninterested in doing the much-needed planning that the business owner needs before an exit and the elevated planning often required after the sale for decades to come.

Since the industry is so profitable, it has no incentive to strive for more, which also leads to a lack of leadership from the wealth advisors and teams.

Outright Greed: It's the Business Model, Not the Wealth Advisor

The incentive to sell a product with a large up-front commission—for example, life insurance and annuities—often means advisors do not operate in the best interest of the family.

I wrote the foreword to a book about wealth management that talked about annuities a fair amount. In my opinion, there are three types of annuities:

1. Evil ones that should never be sold to anybody—they're only good for the broker or the insurance company.
2. Good ones that are sold out of greed for the wrong reasons—they're used inappropriately to make money for the broker.
3. Good ones that are used appropriately and sparingly for the right client in the right situation—an advisor will recommend these only when applicable.

In other words, annuities aren't inherently evil and should not be thrown out of consideration entirely, but they should be structured so that they're more consumer-friendly and used properly.

You might be the client of one of the major Wall Street investment firms and have a really good experience, but it's going to be because you lucked out and got the good broker or advisor. If my company, Questmont, took over your portfolio, the experience would be a gradient better—but it's true that you can have a really good advisor at an institution who works within the toolbox they have.

Our work is to optimize the experience and service, but not all advisors are bad: it's the business model that creates potential conflicts of interest and fails clients, not necessarily always the wealth advisor.

THE CHALLENGE OF STARTING AN INDEPENDENT FIRM

Given the need for fiduciary investment advice undistorted by large company incentives, it would be ideal for advisors to work for truly independent firms like Questmont. However, high start-up costs are one of the biggest problems preventing any new advisor coming into the industry from starting their own firm. This is a difficult hurdle for the individual advisor to overcome because they likely can't afford their own office, their own administrative assistant, or their own compliance officer. Instead, they affiliate with a larger insurance or broker-dealer-based company. As a result, there are fewer investment advisory fiduciary options for high-net-worth families.

Compliance Oversight

Part of the challenge of starting an independent firm is compliance oversight. The legal and practical hurdles to representing the client's interest are substantial and cost potentially hundreds of thousands of dollars a year. If an advisor runs an independent firm, where will they establish custody of their clients' assets under management in a portfolio?

FINANCIAL AND MAINSTREAM MEDIA

One other very important issue that I want to scream from the mountaintop is my naked, open opposition to and distaste for financial media and mainstream media in general. The news should not be different from the truth. It should report the truth. Instead, it often does the opposite, spreading a narrative to the effect that some major financial or economic crisis is happening now, always, and forever. The reason for this pervasive false story is as old as journalism itself and expressed in the tacit principle "If it bleeds, it leads." Over the years, newspaper editors have found that bad news reliably draws the most eyeballs. These days, bad news draws the most clicks.

I think of this phenomenon as the "apocalypse du jour." In every instance, the crisis gets resolved. In fact, it was never a crisis in the first place. In short, the world stubbornly refuses to end. When today's apocalypse shuffles off to insignificance, the media does not announce the passing of the crisis or apologize for making a mountain out of a molehill. They simply go silent, stop reporting on the issue, and then begin rending their garments and shrieking about the next supposedly insurmountable crisis.

Financial journalism is a business; it makes money by selling advertising. It has little interest in helping investors to succeed. Its mandate is fully dispensed and discharged when someone clicks on its content. The organizing principle of financial journalism is to do everything in its power to frighten people into watching their portfolios minute by minute. This dynamic is precisely the problem; journalism cannot allow you, even for a moment, to take a long-term perspective. If you did, you might stop watching or clicking. Since so much of our investing success depends on our ability to tune out the noise and to stick to our wealth plan, it might be said that the ultimate noisemaker of financial journalism is downright opposed to your success.

Thus, the mortal danger to the financial media business is that you will start to relax, feel a little bit better about the market and even the world, and tune it out. The media cannot allow this sense of peace, because if your financial blood pressure declines to normal levels, you will naturally stop clicking on every apocalyptic headline. All else being equal, a calm demeanor and the ability to ignore the chatter will make you a better investor—but that behavior will depress their advertising revenue.

I am reminded of a famous business magazine that put Elizabeth Holmes on its cover, enshrining her as the biotechnology entrepreneur who was later convicted of fraud in connection to her blood-testing company, Theranos. It also named Enron America's most innovative company for six years running, but of course that enterprise also turned out to be a complete fraud. Lots of credibility there, don't you think?

I reiterate: the financial media exists for one reason and one reason only—to sell advertising. Advertising revenues are inextricably linked to clicks and are an absolute function of the extent to which the media can trap readers in a vicious cycle of fear and regret. In short, the financial media exists to help investors fail.

During the great financial crisis of 2008 to 2009, my wife (Sonya) and I decided to have a little fun. We took a stopwatch, poured a glass of wine, and watched the news for how often it reported facts versus speculation. We concluded that broadcasters reported actual news less than 15 percent of the time. The rest was opinion or spin.

COMMON ADVISOR MISTAKES

Now that you understand the larger forces at play in the wealth management industry, including the highly skewed incentives outside of independent firms, let's look at a few of the most common mistakes that ineffective advisors make with client portfolios.

Stock Overlap

A common mistake is for advisors to allow investors to have stock overlap. This phenomenon occurs when a client has purchased or been sold multiple index funds or mutual funds that essentially own exactly the same companies in the same category, such as small-cap growth or large-cap growth. Whether due to ignorance or lack of planning, this situation creates additional risk and often results in lower returns.

For example, just after the financial crisis of 2008, a neighbor and business owner* approached me for an analysis of his wealth plan and portfolio. We discovered that over 60 percent of his funds were invested in the financial sector, which was the hardest hit by the biggest recession since the Great Depression. His lack of awareness caused his portfolio to decline in value by more than 70 percent.

Leakage

Leakage occurs when a wealthy family does not have an advisor who regularly performs stress tests or analytics on their wealth plan. We frequently see families who are overpaying for insurance they no longer need.

For example, a multimillionaire contractor was already retired but still paying $10,000 per year for long-term disability insurance. Additionally, he was paying over $50,000 a year for life insurance policies that were improperly structured and no longer needed.

Simply by analyzing the situation, we were able to redirect over $60,000 of the client's income annually to more productive ventures.

Not Considering All Options

Another problem is many investors are completely unaware of the existence of virtual family offices. This leads to the unfortunate outcome that they over-pay, are underserved, and are taken for granted. An independent fiduciary investment advisor should direct you toward a service you need that they don't necessarily sell themselves.

TIME FOR A CHANGE

In conclusion, the financial advice industry is in desperate need of reform. Too many investors have been burned by advisors more concerned with their own compensation than their clients' best interests. The path to financial security is fraught with land mines, but there is hope: by learning the industry's darkest secrets, investors can empower themselves to navigate the terrain with confidence. It's time to demand better from those entrusted with your financial well-being. The future of effective, ethical wealth management is ours to shape.

CHAPTER 2

THE POTHOLES OF MY LIFE

It all happened so fast. On my fifteenth birthday, June 28, 1979, my life was turned upside down when my family abruptly moved from our idyllic small town in Spring Grove, Pennsylvania, to the suburbs of Orange County, California. I was ripped from my comfortable, close-knit community and dropped into a foreign, affluent environment where I struggled to adapt.

Growing up, I had been the quintessential "good kid"—a talented athlete and artist from a loving, supportive family. My mother taught me I could be or do anything that I wanted. My dad was street-smart and very magnanimous. But the jarring transition to my new high school shook my sense of self.

In the middle of a particularly harsh winter, my parents had decided to look for jobs in a sunny state. Wouldn't you know it? They got an offer to fly to Los Angeles to meet with an engineering company and went for what I thought was going to be a weekend *paid for* by the company. Naively, I thought they were just visiting L.A. under the pretense of interviewing for a job. Instead, Dad was offered and accepted a job—and bought a house—all in a matter of days! My world got upended in a fashion that was unfathomable to me at the time. I was crushed and only had ninety days' notice before my life was ripped apart.

In the fall, I started attending Mission Viejo High School in Orange County, one of the wealthiest counties in the country at the time. We were poor relative to that environment, which was humbling. I was thrown into wealth for the first time. I discovered quickly that I did not fit in: my classmates were hyper-focused on fashion and music, while I clung to my jeans, T-shirts, and conservative Pennsylvanian sensibilities. I felt completely out of place.

REBEL WITHOUT A CAUSE

The anger I felt toward my parents for moving us to Orange County remained latent and undiscovered for many years. Unsure of how to cope, I began to rebel out of anger, and most of my time in Southern California was spent floundering around and partying.

Unconsciously, I began lowering my standards. At school, I started gravitating toward the kids who were the least productive, kids for whom the requirements to hang out were the lowest. Gradually I started spending more time with them, partying, and listening to heavy metal. After about a year, I began to blow off classes, and the unexcused absences started to pile up.

One weekend when my parents were in Denver for a three-day business trip, I wrote a letter claiming I was on the business trip with them and forged my dad's signature. Eventually, this lie came back to bite me. My parents had a meeting with my guidance counselor, who showed them the pile of notes I had signed with my father's name, and they were shocked. That was the beginning of the end of my time living at home.

In 1981 or 1982, I crashed a car after catching my then-girlfriend making out with another guy. Looking back, it was definitely a cry for help, as I was lost and frightened in this scary, big, new world and did not know what to do.

My mother had always been my biggest fan and strongest supporter; she thought I was perfect. However, we began to fight, which ultimately led to me moving out of the house during my senior year. I didn't even have a car. I do not think I had my driver's license yet, but I was rebelling against my parents, so the journey of living on my own and learning began.

I only lasted a week at the local community college before dropping out. I showed up, went to class, made a few bad choices, and quit. I have no shame referring to myself as a big loser; I was just a stupid kid, lost and searching.

In hindsight, I now realize that period also marked the beginning of my resilience, a quality I've drawn upon throughout my career. I was a seventeen-year-old who had moved across the country two years earlier from a small town to a big city. I found the courage—even if it was out of spite and anger—to go out and get an apartment of my own. It was very daring. I lived with my friend Elliott. I went through an ugly period and got into several car accidents.

Looking back, not only have I bounced back from every stumble and challenge, but I have prospered. I have learned how to turn adversity into positive energy and create something better, which would serve me well later in life.

Eventually, I realized I couldn't keep hiding in California. I decided to return to Pennsylvania, where I naively believed I could recapture my former idyllic life—not understanding, or not wanting to understand, that the problem at this point was me. Fortunately, my uncle Tom and aunt Linda had agreed to let me move in with them until I could get an apartment. I lived with them for about three months.

Thanks to Uncle Tom, I got a job selling tires, though I only earned $18,000 to $20,000 a year. Shortly afterward, I discovered that, of course, the temptations hadn't stayed in California. So I continued down a self-destructive path, partying heavily and bouncing between low-wage jobs. With five other guys, I moved into what became a big party house, and eventually, even there, I was no longer welcome.

I ended up renting a small apartment with a guy named Vince, by which point, I had already lost my job selling tires. I took the crappiest job in town, working nights at a trucking station unloading trucks. Freezing in the wintertime on a loading dock, making seven dollars an hour, I felt my life begin to spiral.

ROCK BOTTOM

On January 25, 1987, at twenty-three years old, I invited my friend Mike over to watch the Super Bowl. The New York Giants defeated the Denver Broncos that year, and after the game, we did not want the party to end. There was not much happening on a Sunday night in the small town of York, so we decided, stupidly, to drive ninety miles to Baltimore in the snow to hang out at a bar. At closing time, Mike tried to persuade me to go back home, but I still wanted to keep the party going. He was my ride, and I needed to get back for work the next afternoon. We got into an argument, however, and I told him to buzz off.

I stayed at the bar, where I was trying to pick up an attractive gal. Believing I was making some headway, I thought maybe I could stay with her for the night. Eventually, her boyfriend showed up, and I finally realized how pathetic I was. It was now two in the morning, and I was standing outside in the freezing winter weather, ninety miles from home, with no car, almost no money, and no place to sleep. I wandered around for a while, knowing I needed to find a safe place. I came across a police station. Imagine this: I was stranded, cold, and drunk, and I had drugs in my pocket, yet I had the stupid courage to walk into the police station and ask to sleep on a bench in the waiting room...and they let me!

From the police station, I called Mark Sackett, a kid I knew from Spring Grove. He was younger than I was but had a truly kind heart. In high school, he had been involved in a car accident in which another kid I grew up with died, and Mark had never been the same.

When I reached out and begged for his help, he kindly got in his car, picked me up, and drove my sorry ass back to my small apartment in Pennsylvania. That night was the beginning of an epiphany: I realized I needed to improve my life. I was raised better. I knew better. I could not believe that I was making such stupid decisions.

My parents had long since adopted a tough-love relationship with me, so when I called my dad and asked if I could come home and reboot my life with a little help, he said no. I asked again a week later, and he and my mom agreed to let me move back home, but only if I signed a contract with three provisions: Number one, I would have no rights in their home. Number two, I would get a job immediately, even if it was janitorial. Number three, I would turn over all my financial affairs to them. I agreed immediately and started packing.

WINDOW OF OPPORTUNITY

By March of '87, I was back in California. The best job I could get was working six days a week selling tires. I quit drinking and partying, which was the start of three years of complete sobriety and clarity.

While I worked that job, my dad and I realized I was really good at communicating, and I began to care about helping people. The tiniest little green shoot of good things started to sprout.

I didn't want to go back to college, so my dad encouraged me to get into sales: he suggested cars, real estate, or insurance. I landed a job at a property and casualty insurance agency. The owner also sold life insurance with cash values, IRAs, mutual funds, and annuities. I was exposed to financial services for the first time. I was absolutely fascinated, particularly by the idea that you could pay premiums into a life insurance policy and protect your family while building up a savings plan. I ran straight home after work that night and showed my dad. What a truly exciting moment! He told me to sit down, pulled out his portfolio, and showed me his policies. He already had whole life policies for himself, my mom, my sister, and me.

His insurance agent got me an interview with the general agent, Dick Pohlman, who agreed to give me a shot. I didn't know anything about financial services, life insurance, or how the industry worked. I just knew it was a shining window of opportunity for me. I was intrigued. Now, I had the opportunity to make a decent living selling these commission-based products and funds.

In the early days, my parents really wanted me to have a part-time job, even if it was through a temp agency, because selling life insurance was paid solely on commission. I would be on a construction site breaking up rocks with a sledgehammer one day; the next day, I would be filing and doing secretarial work. Once I started learning the ropes of selling and making cold calls, Dick did me a favor: he told my dad that if my parents forced me to get another temp job, he would fire me. That forced them to back off. To my surprise, I excelled. My natural people skills and ability to really listen to people served me well in sales. I earned around $17,000 the first year and $40,000 the second year. By the third year, I made over $100,000.

I began to rebuild my life. I was enamored and stayed sober for those first three years because I really wanted to make it work. I didn't want to go back to my old life of couch surfing or sleeping in my car or on park benches, with no physical address because I didn't have money to pay the rent. A few short years earlier, if I had money, I would have spent it on partying. My situation had been so dire that cold-calling didn't scare me at all. Picking up the phone and asking one of my father's friends to buy some term life insurance felt easy by comparison. I had no problem making those calls.

AWAKENING

Simultaneously, in 1989, I began dating one of my sister's good friends. We developed a strong connection that evolved too quickly. Emotionally, I was still a child. My maturity was stunted because of my eight-year period of partying. But she was attractive. She was cool. We fell in love. I proposed and she accepted, but neither of us was ready for the reality of marriage. She was only nineteen, and I was twenty-five.

We went on an Alaskan cruise for our honeymoon. It was a rewards trip paid for by the company because I was one of the top sellers of insurance.

On that trip, we met the company's top-earning general agent for the entire states of Pennsylvania and New Jersey. I'll call him Charles. He was the highest-paid agent at that time, more so than my boss, Dick, the general agent of Southern California, who was also on this trip. Charles began what I now realize was a recruitment process. It was subtle at first, but I was too naive to see it. He began sharing his business documents, and it became obvious to me that Dick was an old-school salesman while Charles was more polished, educated, and business-savvy. He effectively recruited my wife and me to come back to Pennsylvania and consider working for him, with the false promise that I would take over his business someday.

What I didn't realize at the time was that for every dollar in commission I made, my management team also made a dollar. When I learned that fact much later, I began to realize the hierarchical pyramid structure of the business. These guys might have liked me, and they might have wanted to help me, but as long as I kept bringing in new clients, they had little incentive to help me grow. Effectively, they had a hand in every agent's pocket, so they were not incentivized to do their own business. Instead, they were incentivized to recruit a lot of people. They really didn't care if those people quit, because the clients and policyholders those people brought on stayed with the company. That situation created a "spaghetti against the wall" mentality. They hired for volume but didn't screen young agents for quality. In fact, only 17 percent of new agents survive.

I didn't have a college education. I owe Dick Pohlman some love and kindness because he did take a risk on me, supported me, and mentored me properly. However, the system was and still is flawed—and I was too dazzled by the promise of the industry to see through it. After the cruise, Charles's recruitment intensified, full-throated. He came to California for a few days. He met my dad, we went to a professional basketball game, and he invited me to come back to Pennsylvania to discuss further.

In the spring of 1992, we began to negotiate what would be a huge change for me. A short time later, my first wife and I agreed to pack up our stellar little condo in Southern California and move to Harrisburg, Pennsylvania. I ripped apart my life and left sunny Southern California, which had not been on my bingo card, but Charles's recruitment process had planted a seed in my mind. We started over, and I had no clue the company would be making so much money from me. I was completely outmaneuvered. At this moment, an awareness began, which has evolved into my firm's mission to defend its clients and take on their problems and concerns as if they were my own.

My years of personal struggle gave me an outsider's perspective. I am not a creature of the industry. I found success by looking for the chinks in its armor. What was the industry doing? What was it delivering, what was missing, and how could I make and provide a better service to my clients? I've always felt as if the industry didn't want me looking too deeply.

If you built your wealth yourself, then maybe you can relate to these challenges. I was not born with a silver spoon. I did not go to college. I was not a legacy hire. I had no leg up, so I have always felt I needed to deliver, deliver, deliver, deliver.

Since I was not allowed in the ivory tower, if I was going to compete, I had to build a tower of my own. This allows me a certain freedom not to be bound by the norms of the industry. I am bound by the client.

CHAPTER 3

WHAT, YOU'RE NOT COORDINATED?

In this chapter, I will explain in full detail the family office concept, its history, how it connects to the history of the financial services industry, and why you should consider it for your own finances. Most importantly, you will leave this chapter understanding how a family office can benefit you beyond what other wealth management services provide. And finally, I'll share a story of a virtual family office in practice.

WHAT IS WEALTH MANAGEMENT?

Money is a tool that can enhance and optimize your life—or hurt your life. It needs to be managed by a competent and benevolent team. Too often, the term "wealth management" is simply a buzzword that my industry has used in the last twenty years to make itself sound more important. It's usually a lie. Our in-house research shows that fewer than 3 percent of licensed advisors deliver wealth management, based on the actual industry definition:

**Wealth Management =
Investment Consulting + Advanced Planning +
Relationship Management**

Investment Consulting

One hundred percent of advisors provide investment consulting, and you are already paying the investment advisory fee. It includes asset allocation and portfolio management, which encompass manager due diligence, risk evaluation, and performance analysis.

Advanced Planning

Roughly 80 percent of advisors claim to do advanced planning, but only 7 percent deliver. Advanced planning includes wealth preservation and wealth transfer, and it can also include tax mitigation, estate and charitable planning, and asset protection.

Relationship Management

The final piece entails managing the entire family and all their advisors (tax, legal, insurance, wealth, etc.) in one coordinated team. Your advisor needs to know

Wealth Management Formula

3%

Approx. 3% of advisors nationwide deliver this piece of the formula.

RELATIONSHIP MANAGEMENT

Expert Team Coordination and High-Level Service

7%

80% of advisors claim to do this, but only 7% deliver.

ADVANCED PLANNING

Wealth Preservation and Wealth Transfer

Wealth Enhancement and Charitable Giving

Provided by Questmont at No Additional Fee

100%

100% of advisors do this. It's table stakes.

INVESTMENT CONSULTING

Asset Allocation and Portfolio Management

Manager Due Diligence, Risk Evaluation, and Performance Analysis

Investment Advisory Fee

(You are already paying this.)

the type of investor you are. They need to know this human side before they can advise on the money itself. Relationship management should be at the core of the service of a great advisor. A true wealth advisor coordinates all the team members to get them in a room, be it virtual or in person, to solve the client's problem.

I love asking potential clients, "When was the last time your 'wealth advisor,' CPA, attorney, and insurance agent got together and worked on nothing but solving your problems and concerns?" The answer is almost always "Well, that never happens." That teamwork represents true wealth management. And indeed, approximately only 3 percent of advisors nationwide deliver this piece of the formula.

In short, we are advising the *wealthy*, not the wealth.

WHAT IS THE ROLE OF A WEALTH ADVISOR?

A true advisor works *with* the client, managing their expectations, their dreams, their goals, and their behavior to be effective. Humans are fundamentally flawed investors because they often make investments based on emotion rather than history, facts, or process. For example, if you want to buy a yacht or a bigger mansion, or give more money to charity, we have a tool to help you make reasonable projections regarding the financial markets and what will be possible. We manage our client's expectations of their investments. It's behavioral investment counseling. In essence, certain *behaviors* are what people can't afford. Managing your financial behavior is a form of life optimization, which is a tool that I will explain in greater detail in Chapter 7.

One couple owned multiple health practices and commercial real estate investments and decided to divorce. We represented the wife, who was not as involved in the day-to-day running of the health practices and had never experienced great amounts of liquidity before. As part of the divorce settlement, her ex bought out her share of these assets, giving her a huge cash windfall.

Contrary to the wealth plan that was laid out and our best advice, she immediately bought a beachfront investment property. I use the term "investment property" loosely, because she clearly intended it to be her second home most of the time. In her mind, she had sold a business for $30 million and thought she could buy a property for $5 million. But her dreams-to-grounding ratio was terribly off, and within a year, she chose to sell the beach property and regain liquidity, which proved wise in ensuring her future.

The reality is, clients don't always follow our advice, and she regretted it. This story illustrates the importance of having a written wealth plan in the first place, as well as the risks and dangers of not following it. The plan is always based on the client's desires, dreams, and goals. However, those are carefully compared to the finite assets and resources of that family, so that my team can provide them with leadership, not just advice on what they can and cannot afford and what they should and should not do. It also highlights the fallibility of human beings and why they need thoughtful but tough love and leadership regarding their wealth.

If the person who manages your money calls themselves a wealth advisor, then chances are their clients are already wealthy, which means it's the human side they need to focus on. So yes, the money needs management, but ultimately the money is just the toolbox to optimize your life. At Questmont, the primary focus with our client families, their children, and their grandchildren is on the human side, helping them align their wealth with their values in the most efficient way. In the chapters that follow, I will share tools and solutions we provide so that you have the necessary knowledge to hire the right wealth advisor.

WHAT IS A FAMILY OFFICE?

As I mentioned in Chapter 1, a family office is an entity that wealthy people use to off-load the responsibility and headaches of managing their wealth. As best we can tell, the first example of a family office was the king's steward.[4] Dating back to medieval Europe, this role oversaw all the king's lands and holdings and was responsible for the day-to-day management and financial affairs of the royal household.

A more modern example of a family office would be the Rockefellers, who started the first known single-family office. As wealth has exploded in the United States, the family office model has evolved. When a family's net worth is $250 million or more, they may want to consider forming their own family office, as Bill Gates did.

---

[4] John Pierpont Morgan, "Family Offices: A History of Stewardship," *Financial Times*, Oct. 19, 2017, https://www.ft.com/content/403a2cb4-a9cb-11e7-ab66-21cc87a2edde.

At the single-family office level, a major part of the offering is to coordinate support and administrative services that address myriad issues, including the following:

- ensuring tax compliance
- providing audit defense
- overseeing state and gift tax execution
- developing and updating a family balance sheet
- providing budgets that include income and cash flow statements
- paying bills
- providing general ledger reports
- tracking and reporting investments that include cost and tax basis
- administering an estate
- monitoring special collections, such as art, wine, or cars
- tracking the days in the country for tax purposes

In the health area:

- providing 24/7 on-call physicians
- offering complete case continuity through a qualified position that coordinates all the specialists' telephone diagnoses and treatments

In the security area:

- protecting privacy
- maintaining cybersecurity
- providing personal protection
- ensuring travel safety
- conducting security investigations and due diligence

Special projects:

- buying an island
- facilitating an adoption
- facilitating admissions to a private club
- restoring the identity of a family member after a company was hacked

Effectively, the family office concept is a brain trust. You need tax advice, both preparation and forward planning. In many cases, you need business analytics and business advice if the wealth came from a business. You need an attorney or legal advice, asset allocation advice and protection, insurance advice, and portfolio management.

When you move up the wealth stream, a family office can become more complex to address specialized services related to concierge medicine, private jets, yachts, travel, house staff, and so forth. If your sense of self comes from a business that you plan to sell or retire from, you might even need life transition counseling. The family office needs the wisest, most intelligent, and well-vetted professionals in each class. Even at the single-family office level, recent research has shown that only 20 percent are high-functioning. Sixty percent are functioning, and 20 percent are substandard.[5]

---

[5] Angelo Robles, foreword to *How to Build a High-Performing Single-Family Office: Guidelines for Family Members and Senior Executives*, Robert Daugherty and Russ Alan Prince (Tampa: Gatekeeper Press, 2021), x.

MULTIFAMILY OFFICE SERVICES

For people who do not have billions, there is the structure of a multifamily office, which represents multiple families. Less complex or lower levels of wealth don't need a single-family office, so a multifamily office fills the same role and is likely the better solution. In the town where I was born, there was a multifamily office started by seven wealthy families, and that office only represented those seven families.

WHAT IS A VIRTUAL FAMILY OFFICE?

Explaining what we do and having people understand it quickly is hard. On the one hand, titling ourselves a virtual family office is a differentiator. On the other, if a potential client doesn't know what that term means, their mind goes down the wrong path.

One person thought we were business brokers or investment bankers who help people sell their business. While we're part of that process, we're not the ones who actually sell it. We help them coordinate the process. Another family thought that virtual meant only Zoom meetings, when in fact the word "virtual" refers to services that are outsourced to an external firm, rather than having an in-house team. The virtual family office model was developed in the 1990s by Michael T. Hartley: it is a multifamily office without our clients having to keep a CPA, attorney, or investment banker permanently on their payroll; instead, we pull them in as needed on an ad hoc basis.

My company specializes in working with business owners to help them exit their businesses. The problem is that many people don't even know that transition experts exist. Instead of enjoying the success of their life's work, they're often stressed out and feel taken advantage of.

In 2010, I hired a firm called CEG Worldwide, which evolved from a coaching and consulting group into a mastermind group. We meet in person annually in California and online once a month. Today, we also underwrite research on wealthy families, family offices, and advisors who serve them or (in many cases) underserve them. My journey to building what we refer to as a virtual family office started at this stage.

Collectively, my team recognized that many families are underserved by the existing wealth management and financial advice structures. I saw the need for a coordinated and collaborative leadership and advice model, which led to adopting the *virtual* family office model. The demand for this outsourced solution seemed obvious. In conjunction with several of my CPA colleagues, we built a team that included a law firm, a CPA firm, my wealth management firm, and an insurance brokerage. This was the most economical solution to serving the needs of business owners and wealthy families without our clients having to keep all the team members on a payroll.

The Business Owners Resource Alliance

The Business Owners Resource Alliance (BORA) is a key component of the virtual family office team. The leaders of each of the firms on the team develop deep personal relationships. There must be connection, trust, alignment, and a bond among those high-level partners, or it simply does not work.

The process becomes highly bespoke. When a wealthy family already has advisors who are highly qualified and competent, such as an estate-planning attorney or a CPA, we plug them into the planning process and coordinate with them, as opposed to having the client use the CPA firm or estate attorney on our team.

This approach means that every single client has a different customized team, which makes running the virtual family office and staying on top of the client's family issues very detail-oriented and extremely white glove. The members of a VFO develop a powerful relationship, work in congruence, and then effectuate the plans together.

Protecting Your Interests If You Become Incapacitated

Imagine you've sold your contracting business and you and your spouse are happily enjoying your retirement. You're enjoying spending time with your children and your grandchildren, giving money to further your grandchildren's education, and donating money to your church and charities locally that you've loved all your life. Then imagine that, sadly, your spouse, who is in his seventies, begins to fade and slowly dies of natural causes.

You are left on your own. Although you have loving children and grandchildren, this change of circumstance forces you to downsize and move out of the home you have loved for decades. During this process, you get into a horrific car accident; someone hits you, and you're unconscious for nearly six months—fighting for your life, unable to speak, in a coma.

Your children don't know who your power of attorney is, where you bank, or what insurance coverages you have. They have no way of paying your bills or maintaining both homes since you were in the process of moving.

Close your eyes and picture the havoc, the pain, and the infighting that could erupt among your children because they are scared. They mean well and want to help, but you've left them with no toolbox.

Now, imagine the same circumstances, the same six months unconscious and fighting for your life, except in this case, you have a virtual family office service that you've been working with for several years.

The moment the accident happens, your children reach out to the family financial director, who has become a close friend and knows all the details about your life. He has mourned the loss of your husband with you and attended his funeral. When the emergency occurs, he takes immediate action. The virtual family office has already coordinated your CPA, your legal affairs, and your insurance, and it is immediately able to create some liquidity so that your children can pay your bills, bring forth the powers of attorney, and determine which of the children will be in charge.

Further, the virtual family office is aware of and immediately invokes the proper medical and disability or long-term care insurance to begin paying some of the bills. Since the family office works in partnership with your accountant, your taxes get filed on time, even though you are unconscious during tax-filing season. On the financial side, your family is able to proceed seamlessly. Yes, their hearts are broken. Yes, they're crushed. However, financial and logistical concerns have been completely removed because you made a wise decision several years prior. You overcame your own inertia and fired the large investment firm you were with, which was not coordinating your financial affairs.

This is the power and value of a virtual family office. The thought experiment above is based on a true story that happened to one of our clients. Thankfully, she came out of that coma and, despite her injuries, was happy to be alive, happy to see her children, thrilled to see her grandchildren, and able to begin life anew.

What BORA Does

Proverbs 4:7 says, "Wisdom is the principal thing; therefore get wisdom: and with all thy getting, get understanding." In the process of establishing my firm, it occurred to me that information becomes the enemy. Today more than ever, there are massive amounts of information available to business owners and investors, but there is no understanding. And information without wisdom is a problem. It's very important for successful business owners to filter out irrelevant information and turn the relevant information into usable, actionable wisdom. The role of the family office is to create wisdom from the massive amounts of information out there.

We serve a broad range of families with a net worth ranging from $20 million to $150 million. They can't afford nor do they need to have attorneys, CPAs, and evaluation experts on their payroll. Instead, they hire a wealth manager—my firm. We take responsibility for coordinating and managing all of the advanced planning for their wealth, taxes, legal issues, evaluation needs, and insurance.

Here is the key difference from typical advisors: we also coordinate all of the other "relationship management." We take responsibility for vetting the best professionals in the land—including attorneys, accountants, and insurance people—and negotiating discounts or front-of-the-line services. One of my team members calls this latter benefit a "fast pass." When a client hires us, they are paying the same asset management and planning fees as all our competitors but receiving a much higher level of service, expertise, and benefit.

If a client hires us and does not have a highly qualified CPA, business attorney, or investment banker, it is our responsibility to bring that professional to the table and have no "horse in that race." In other words, we do not get kickbacks or participate in that professional's revenue; it is a purely fiduciary referral. If the client already has these professionals, it is our job to plug our services in with them. Often, a client will have a qualified business attorney or CPA who should not be replaced. We make sure that the CPA talks to the business attorney and the insurance person, which is an extremely labor-intensive process. Plenty of advisors talk a big game and say that they deliver that level of coordination, but few follow through.

The entire BORA team meets virtually once a month to collaborate with our clients on processes such as selling businesses. Then once per quarter, this team meets in person. My wealth management firm takes responsibility for running and funding these in-person meetings, which are free to the clients. The team gives high-quality advice to the wealth management firm's clients. That is the engine that drives this outsourced family office.

My client does not have to pay these experts directly until—this is key—they actually use them to execute a transaction, such as updating a will, creating a trust, or selling a business. In the interim, they are getting the sector's best expertise from a formal team, through a formal process designed with their best interests in mind. The VFO can deliver this experience at a level that I can definitively say these families have never seen previously in their financial lives.

It took years for us to select the right professionals, and it is exceedingly difficult to put a team like this together because they have to want to collaborate, they have to want to grow their businesses, and they have to have the bandwidth. Because these professionals are in high demand, many in the field do not have the time to commit to a team up front. So it takes knowledge and a quality network to execute the difficult process of selecting the right people at the right stage of their careers. They must have availability yet already be well established, with a great reputation in the community in which they operate. Sometimes a team member retires or moves, or their professionals get so busy that they no longer have the bandwidth to contribute, in which case my firm is responsible for efficiently finding a worthy replacement.

I have personally run several BORA teams, including two in Pennsylvania and now two in Florida.

Over time, the teams evolve, which makes the entire VFO concept complex to run and support, explaining why there are so few in existence. We must constantly be vetting other professionals in the event that someone drops off.

Best Practices

Some of the other important best practices at all levels of family offices are creating flexible structures, integrating investment and advanced planning to mitigate tax drag, and evaluating investment managers on an after-tax and fee basis.

Let's say you bought a set of golf clubs for $1,300 in addition to the yearly membership fee for the golf and country club. What if, for that same exact fee, you got a set that helped you drive the ball fifty yards farther, with much more accuracy as well as more attention from the golf pro? You're paying the same. Which one would you choose? The VFO business model is the equivalent of those better clubs, for the same investment as a lackluster "wealth manager." My firm is positioned to deliver more for effectively the same price as (or less than) what most ultra-high-net-worth families are probably already paying.

It took me a long time to realize clients are almost always paying as much as or more than what we charge, so our value proposition is simply that we do more. We provide more value. The challenge for me is letting those clients know, "Hey, you've got a terrible set of clubs because the salesperson worked for the golf and country club. They weren't an independent consultant; they sold you the only set of golf clubs they had to sell."

CHALLENGES UHNW FAMILIES FACE

Ultra-high-net-worth families tend to have a set of challenges in common, which a well-run family office can help address.

Managing Heirs

Developing an asset protection plan that carefully weighs the degree of control relinquished against the potential threat is very important, as is providing education to heirs to prepare them for the responsibility of wealth. We often see children causing problems even with the best of intentions. It is not that the children are being deceptive or ruthless; they are just out of their league.

Heirs in need of support structures can fall into two categories: 1) bad seeds, or 2) well-intentioned but dysfunctional. Many ultra-wealthy families have a tough time reining in manipulative, disruptive, or oppressive family members. Usually, the virtual family office manager can easily identify family members who are pulling down the organization.

The bad seeds tend to become apparent over time. When they engage in regular subterfuge, at a minimum, a great deal of acrimony ensues. These family members are often self-absorbed and commonly feel entitled, habitually expecting, if not demanding, preferential treatment. I will go over personality types in a later chapter. For now, suffice it to say we are highly experienced in working with family members and heirs who run the gamut of personalities and motivations and who need a wide range of guardrails.

How to Outsource

Another challenge these families face is how much management they should outsource. There is a simple formula that can be used:

$$(\text{Frequency} + \text{Complexity}) / (\text{Cost} + \text{Exclusivity}) = \text{Need for Outsourcing}$$

If something is going to be used frequently, you may want to have it in-house or outsource it when you need it.

The questions when choosing a virtual family office versus a single-family office are: How wealthy are you, and what services do you really want to have full-time rather than just on a rare occasion?

If your net worth is $50 million, you don't need those services in house; $100 million is very different from $1 billion, and $10 million is very different from $100 million. And while yes, $20 million is a lot of money, you're not going to buy a private island with $20 million. You can't even afford your own jet. You can charter occasionally, and maybe use NetJets, but you're not going to have your own jet. At $50 million, you can probably have your own jet.

Whatever your situation, the important thing is to have a team of experts who can guide you through the challenges, people who prioritize your best interests and understand the most effective financial strategy for your personality type.

CHAPTER 4

DISCOVERING YOUR HIGH-NET-WORTH PERSONALITY

At Questmont, the essential first step that we always employ to help someone overcome their inertia or fear of change is to have them identify their high-net-worth personality. We all have unconscious patterns that influence how we think, feel, and act around money, and those patterns can impact our income and our lives.

Clients take our proprietary test, which immediately illuminates what is truly important to them about their wealth. Is it having a means to protect their family? Is it funding a favorite charity, living a VIP lifestyle, or something else? In this chapter, I will provide an overview of the nine proven high-net-worth personalities.

FAMILY STEWARDS

Good financial management lets me take good care of my family.

The largest group of affluent individuals, Family Stewards' primary financial concern is taking care of their families. Most of their financial goals and needs are linked to larger family issues such as paying for college or transferring wealth to the next generation. They have an average knowledge of wealth management.

Family Stewards are highly responsive to a variety of advanced planning services because of their motivation to do the best by their families. They readily understand why planning would put them in a better financial position. As a result, they are very interested in estate and financial planning, and most are very interested in asset allocation services.

INDEPENDENTS

To me, successful financial management means freedom.

Independents are straightforward: they value the freedom to do whatever they want, and they seek to achieve this freedom through financial security. While they may hold corporate jobs or run businesses, they dream of financial freedom that would allow them to pursue hobbies or travel full-time.

PHOBICS

The last thing I want to talk about is my money.

Because they so dislike dealing with money, Phobics are hard to miss. They do not understand money, nor do they want to learn about it. Instead, they much prefer delegating the management of their financial affairs to a trusted wealth manager. Because they have little financial expertise with which to judge an advisor, they do so emotionally, going with their "gut feelings."

While most Phobics do need advanced planning services, they are not interested in participating in extensive financial, estate, investment, or tax planning processes. This creates a challenge: getting them to commit to a process they need but do not want to participate in.

THE ANONYMOUS

My money is my business and no one else's.

The Anonymous are intensely private people who do not want to disclose their financial positions to anyone. While this clearly represents a challenge to a wealth manager, since we do need some information to coordinate services, it can also be a plus in my industry. In part because the Anonymous do not want to share information unless absolutely necessary, they tend to be loyal to advisors who have won their trust.

Because they are so tight-lipped about their holdings, many of the Anonymous have not been through basic estate and tax planning processes. However, these advanced planning services are appropriate for the Anonymous personality.

MOGULS

Being rich means having power.

Moguls are activated by power. They seek control, influence, and power in their families, businesses, communities, and finances. While they do have some financial knowledge, they are not interested in finances per se. Rather, they regard it as another forum for flexing their power and control.

Moguls find the idea of asset allocation very appealing. It means they can have control over the high-level design of their portfolio without having to be involved in the day-to-day details. Because they see themselves as important, prominent people who may be likely targets for lawsuits, they are also very interested in wealth protection.

VIPS

There are lots of ways to get respect, and having money is one of them.

VIPs are status-oriented, enjoying prestige and the respect of others. VIPs are the type of affluent people who look rich, and wealth management for them is about the ability to buy status and possessions.

VIPs are not especially knowledgeable about finances and will rely on wealth management experts for advice. To relate well to VIPs, wealth managers need to be particularly attentive and responsive, while also highlighting the reputation and prestige of their institution or firm.

VIPs often already have financial or estate plans and therefore are not very interested in them. Instead, because they see themselves as minor celebrities who need to protect themselves from lawsuits, their strongest interest is in wealth protection services. They are also interested in charitable giving because they see donations to various causes as a way to elevate their social standing.

ACCUMULATORS

You can never be too rich or too thin, but being rich matters more.

Accumulators save more than they spend, tend to live well below their means, and do not exhibit any outward displays of wealth (and have disdain for those who do). What they do enjoy is watching their money grow. The more they have, the better they feel. Capital appreciation is an end in itself.

Accumulators are open to various advanced planning services, especially if those services will result in more money. Asset allocation services are also attractive to them because the point of asset allocation is to maximize long-term results.

GAMBLERS

You have better odds playing the market than gambling in Vegas.

Gamblers love the excitement and drama of investing. For Gamblers, investing is at least a hobby. For some it is their work, and for a few it is their life. As a result, they are more performance-sensitive than any other group. While they are very knowledgeable about investing, they are not always astute. They believe, for example, that it is possible to consistently beat the market. Not surprisingly, they often have a higher-than-usual risk tolerance.

Gamblers love to find people with whom they can talk about investing and need their wealth managers to be as involved as they are. They like their wealth managers to share in the emotional excitement of investing and want them to have the same level of investing expertise.

Most Gamblers are not particularly interested in having someone approach them with advanced planning services unless such services are truly state of the art.

INNOVATORS

Derivatives are the best thing that ever happened.

Innovators are extremely knowledgeable and like to be on the cutting edge of wealth management. They like new products, innovative services, and sophisticated analytical methods. They often have technical backgrounds and might be computer programmers, engineers, or mathematicians.

The Nine High-Net-Worth Personalities

1. Family Stewards
- Focused on taking care of their families
- Conservative in personal knowledge and professional life
- Not very knowledgeable about investing

2. Independents
- Seek the personal freedom money makes possible
- Feel investing is a means to an end
- Not interested in the process of investing or wealth management

3. Financial Phobics
- Confused and frustrated by the responsibility of wealth
- Dislike managing finances and avoid technical discussions of it
- Choose advisors based on the level of personal trust

4. Anonymous
- Primarily concerned with confidentiality
- Prize privacy for their financial affairs
- Likely to concentrate assets with an advisor who protects them

5. Moguls
- Primarily concerned with control
- Value investing as another way of extending personal power
- Decisive in decisions; rarely look back

6. VIPs
- Value investing for the ability to purchase status possessions
- Care about prestige
- Like to affiliate with institutions and advisors with leading reputations

7. Innovators
- Focused on leading-edge products and services
- Sophisticated, with an appreciation for complex products
- Tend to be tech-savvy and highly educated

8. Accumulators
- Focused on making their portfolios bigger
- Want performance-oriented investments
- Tend to live below their means and spend frugally

9. Gamblers
- Enjoy investing for the excitement of it
- Tend to be very knowledgeable and involved
- Exhibit a high risk tolerance

To earn the trust and assets of Innovators, an effective wealth manager will prove their worth in terms of leading-edge product expertise. It is not unusual for Innovators to run sophisticated analytical software on their own.

Like Gamblers, Innovators are interested in only the most sophisticated planning services. If a wealth advisor conducts an asset allocation analysis, they should be prepared to review and explain the various assumptions built into the model used.

KNOWING YOUR PERSONALITY HELPS

Our personality survey offers a great tool to help our clients better manage wealth, since it allows them to better understand themselves. People seldom score in only one category; it's more common to score in two or three. For instance, if you're a Phobic, that won't be your only defining trait; you'll be a Phobic *and* a Family Steward or a Phobic *and* an Independent. Chances are, you already have a general sense of your financial personality but just haven't labeled it.

I score fairly high on VIP: I like driving really nice cars and having beautiful things. However, I also score very high on Family Steward, which means I have a strong desire to take care of the important people in my life with that money: my wife, my son, my little sister, and everyone who works at my firm.

What I have learned about myself—and this helps me with my clients—is that my whole nature is contrarian. I score pretty high on Mogul, which means I want a lot of personal power. I want to use money as a way to control my personal circumstances, rather than allowing some-one else to control them. For example, I hate traveling via commercial airlines, dealing with the TSA and the lay-overs. My inner Mogul loves flying private. It gives me control over when and how I leave and how I arrive.

Recently, my wife and I were on a holiday cruise. There were eighty other people on board a two-hundred-foot ship. We were told what time to eat, what time to disembark to the island, and which beaches we could visit. Moguls do not wait for the tenders on their chartered boats to tell them what time they can go to shore. Moguls tell the tenders what time to go to shore. I strive to be able to afford the yacht and to be the captain myself so that I—not a big charter company—can decide which beach we're going to go to, what time to leave, where to dock, and what's on the menu.

Tailoring Services

Not only does personality type tell us a lot about our clients' unique approaches to having money, we also use that information to create a customized experi-ence. You're born with these traits, and no amount of wealth planning is going to change them. However, we can implement strategies to work with your embed-ded traits.

Let's say we have someone who is an Anonymous; when they come into our office, we will rush them into a conference room so that no one else will see them, because their privacy is a core part of their personality.

With a Phobic, it's important for us to know that we have to put a strong plan in place up front, because they're probably not going to engage much. One of our clients sold a business for $70 million and ultimately ended up getting divorced. We were able to identify through the personality test and our early exploratory meeting that he was a high Phobic. This was a classic case of fear, inertia, and simply not wanting to deal with his finances. He previously had an advisor who was a solo practitioner, not offering a coordinated family office experience, but was charging him over $100,000 a year.

When he explained his experience to us, he said he was confused. He did not understand investing or wealth management and felt talked down to. We uncovered legions of mistakes and shortcomings in his planning, which had caused him to pay excess money every year in taxes as well as high fees on illiquid and poorly managed hedge funds. The previous advisor had also set up an asset protection plan that was locking up millions of dollars of money that he needed for his current income. Being a Phobic had hurt this client. He needed to find a better advisory team. He knew that he had outgrown the advisor he was with, including his CPA and lawyer, but his phobic nature was costing him several hundred thousand dollars a year in overpayments on insurance, taxes, and investments.

A Great Marital Tool

Knowing your high-net-worth personality is also a great marital tool. I like to joke with clients that if they don't know their personality type, they won't get along with their spouse as well. Understanding your spouse's personality can also help you have more productive conversations about money and ultimately inform your financial decisions.

For example, we have clients who are husband and wife. The husband scores high as a Family Steward, and the wife scores very high as an Accumulator. A dilemma came up recently in which their life insurance premium was due. It was substantial, and it was set up years ago to cover estate costs because of the size of their taxable estate. The client's mother is also wealthy and had stopped paying premiums on her life insurance policy, which is in a trust, and was requesting that her three children take over payment of her premiums. When we ran our cash flow and stress test numbers, we found they could clearly afford and should continue to pay both premiums. However, this created tension between the spouses, given their different high-net-worth personalities.

The husband's Family Steward nature causes him to gladly want to pay the premiums to have peace. His mother created millions of dollars of additional tax-free cash for his family, including his children.

The wife's Accumulator nature causes her to be concerned about the drain on their cash reserves, even though they have millions of dollars. The concern is simply due to her high-net-worth personality.

Their values are extremely consistent on nearly everything. This was the first time I had ever seen a disagreement between them. When I was counseling them, they were able to come to a happy resolution by recognizing that they have different high-net-worth personalities and meeting in the middle.

Better Understanding Your Business Partner

This tool also works very effectively for business partners who are able to approach the wealth of the business differently. For example, if your proclivity is toward being a Family Steward, you can consider how your goals align with and diverge from a partner who is a Phobic and really doesn't like dealing with wealth or an Anonymous who loves being wealthy but is extremely private.

In addition to helping your advisors serve you better by creating a bespoke experience, understanding your high-net-worth personality and that of your spouse and your business partners helps ensure your team can create a truly effective plan to keep you happy, aligned, and on track with your goals.

AMPLIFY GENERATIONAL STABILITY

My grandfather was the only entrepreneur in my world. He had the courage to start a furniture and appliance business out of his home during World War II, but he was neither wealth savvy nor succession savvy. Despite his best intentions, he made some very poor business decisions that impacted our family's unity.

He and my grandmother had five children, spanning fifteen years between oldest and youngest. He brought his eldest son into the business, and while that helped him grow and manage the business and have "skin in the game," he did not allow his three middle children to work in the business or have an ownership stake, because they were daughters.

Later, he brought his youngest son into the business and gave him equal opportunity and ultimately equal ownership, despite the eldest son having already worked in the business for fifteen years. My grandfather had nobody to advise him or shine a spotlight on the inequality his decision created or the fact that it sent his son the message that his first fifteen years of effort were not valuable.

In addition, by not bringing his three daughters into the business, he created some dissent among his grandchildren. As a grandchild of one of those daughters, I did not have equal access to, rights to, or inheritance of the family possessions. In the end, the situation created animosity, confusion, selfishness, and distrust among his five children.

Twenty-five years later, when my wife and I attended a family function, though my grandparents were long since deceased, the battle raged on. Their children were still bickering over an asset that had been liquidated a quarter century prior. Rather than creating love, harmony, and the desire to do good things for the world, my grandfather inadvertently created the opposite.

In this chapter, I will outline the importance of amplifying generational stability. As the amount of global wealth has exploded in the past decade, affluent families are increasingly facing the problems of great wealth. They do not wish to raise irresponsible, entitled children; rather, they desire to use their wealth to make an impact on the world and share their values with future generations.

The family office is a key component of amplifying generational stability for multiple reasons. They include family education and writing family constitutions, as well as astute and responsible estate planning so that children are not given control over too much wealth too quickly.

The family office takes the long view, which is looking beyond the founders' generation into the next generations.

NO SPOILED KIDS!

As a result of having witnessed too many families with either dysfunctional children or unhappy relationships due to their great levels of wealth, part of Questmont's three-step method is to amplify generational stability. We have discovered that the creator of that wealth is typically the first generation. If the creator of that wealth spoils their children, four things are fairly predictable:

- Doing so creates entitled children.
- They will likely not pass that good fortune to the third generation.
- They certainly will not use it for the greater good.
- They will probably be unlikable assholes.

Therefore, during the part of the process focused on amplifying generational stability, it is important for the family to identify their goals very thoroughly. With the involvement of the children, we help them create a family constitution, a four-page guiding document for what is really important to the family.

BEHAVIORAL INVESTMENT COUNSELING

One of the other pieces that is especially important is what we call behavioral investment counseling. Behavioral investment counseling acknowledges the fact that human beings, by their nature, are not typically good investors in public markets. They cannot handle the volatility of the market rising and falling. They are driven by fear and greed as opposed to intentional and thoughtful decision-making. In other words, most Americans are bad investors because they're emotional. They cannot stay the course of investing in the stock market in an average year.

Let's just say I pick a fund and invest money in it. Let's say that fund has an average annual return of 10 percent.

This chart of the DALBAR Study shows the under-performance by individual investors due to their own behavior compared to the potential market returns—and what this costs them over time.

The DALBAR research has proven that if we track performance over three, five, ten, twenty, and thirty years, most of the people who bought that original fund are only going to average a 6 or 7 percent rate of return. Why is that? The answer is simple: they didn't stay in it. They jumped in and out. As a result, they underperformed the markets and their own investments because they lacked discipline and let fear and greed dominate.

The average investor without a tough-love wealth advisor—or what we call a behavioral investment counselor—may have awful rates of return due to letting their emotions dictate their behavior.

The DALBAR Study

Average Equity Fund Investor vs. Indexes
Over 30 Years (1/1/1994 - 12/31/2023)

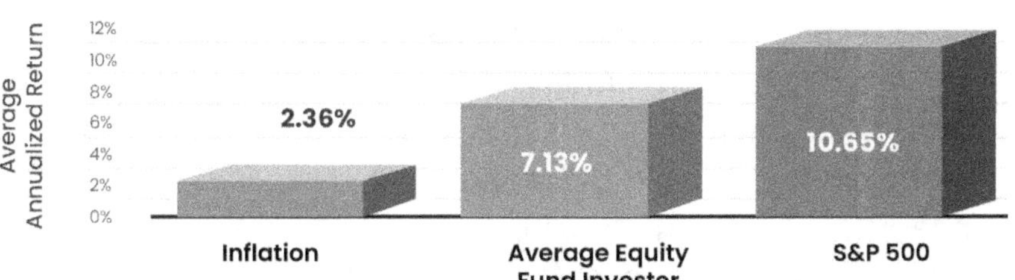

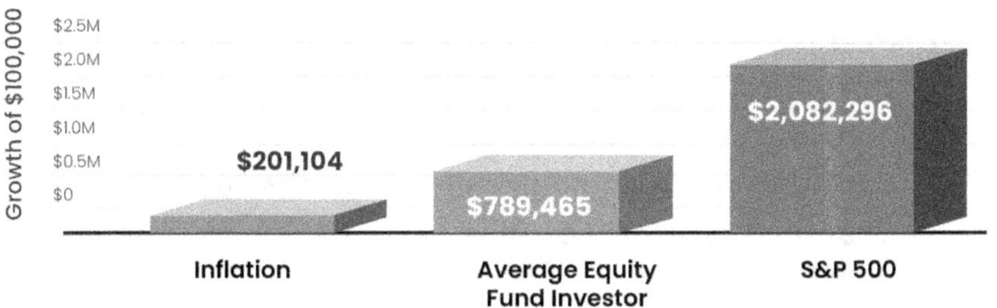

LIFEBOAT DRILL

At Questmont, we solve many of these common mistakes through a tool called a lifeboat drill, which helps ensure our clients don't end up being "DALBAR Dunces." We run every new client through this process, and frequently revisit it with long-term clients. It is a remarkably simple exercise.

We show them chart number one, which we refer to as "investing with your head." It displays the long-term growth of stocks, including large caps, small caps, bonds, and inflation.

For example, small U.S. companies have averaged nearly a 12 percent return, and large companies a 10 percent return, over twenty-, thirty-, fifty-, and one-hundred-year periods. It becomes obvious when looking at the first chart that to maximize returns, money in the stock market must remain in the stock market for long periods of time, preferably decades.

The second chart we refer to as "investing with your heart."

This much more granular chart shows the stock market's annual returns. For example, in 1980, the stock market was down by negative 17 percent in the middle of the year, but if you kept your money in through the entire year, it finished up a positive 26 percent. In fact, the U.S. stock market, as measured by the Standard and Poor's (S&P) 500 index, has an average negative period of 14 percent yearly.

What we have discovered when it comes to investing in public markets is that investors, generally speaking, are motivated by fear and greed. So, we deploy this lifeboat drill at the beginning of every relationship. I often

Investing with Your Head

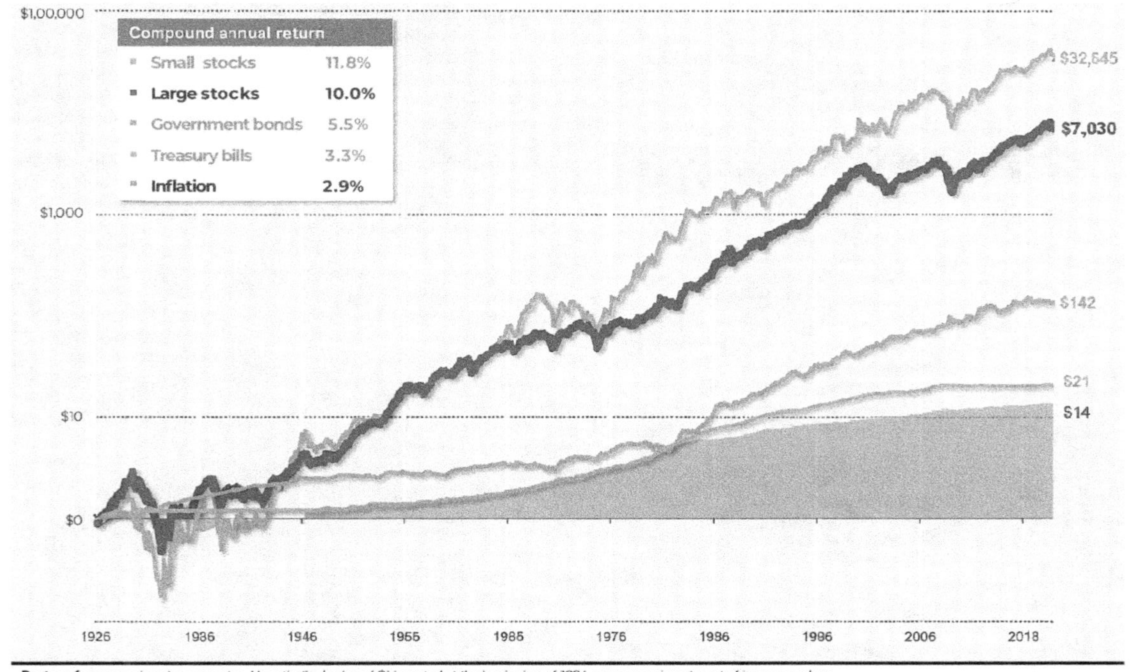

Past performance is not a guarantee. Hypothetical value of $1 invested at the beginning of 1926, assumes reinvestment of income and no transaction costs or taxes. This is for illustrative purposes only and not indicative of any investment. Investments cannot be made directly in an index. ©2019 Morningstar. All Rights Reserved. Methodology in 2019 Ibbotson SBBI Yearbook by Roger G. Ibbotson with Cutts & PNCBS contributing.

Investing with Your Heart

S&P intra-year declines vs. calendar year returns
Despite average intra-year drops of 14.0%, annual returns were positive in 32 of 42 years.

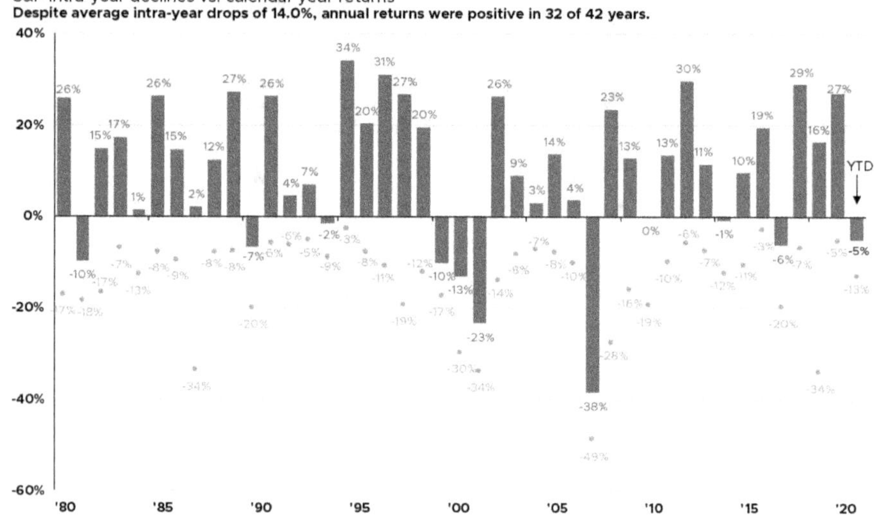

Source: FactSet, Standard & Poor's, J.P. Morgan Asset Management.
Returns are based on the price index only and do not include dividends. "Intra-year drops" refers to the largest market declines from a peak to a trough during the year. This data is provided for illustrative purposes only. The returns shown are calendar year returns from 1980 to 2021, during which the average annual return was 9.4%.
Guide to the Markets — U.S. Data as of March 31, 2022.

tell clients the drill is similar to the safety procedure demonstration, known as a muster drill, that all passengers are required to attend within the first few hours on board a ship. The captain of your ship informs you where the life jackets are, even though you may never need them—and long before you hit an iceberg. As a result, our clients have superior returns over time compared to the general investing public.

Let me share with you the results when a long-term behavioral approach is not used, and the lifeboat drill is not deployed.

In the late '90s through 2009, the best-returning mutual fund was the CGM Focus Fund. It had an average annual return of 48.2 percent. However, the average person who invested in that fund experienced a negative 11 percent return.[6] The only possible explanation—and it's obvious—is that the investors in that fund were jumping in and out and timing it terribly.

Recently, a very famous set of funds named the ARK Funds, run by Cathie Wood, was declared by Morningstar to be the greatest wealth-destroying vehicle over the last ten years. Investors in those funds lost $14.3 billion, which is a result of two factors. One, people jumped in and out of the fund and effectively speculated, rather than behaving like long-term investors. And two, the fund itself has been extremely volatile, experiencing losses ranging from negative 26.38 percent in 2020 to

---

[6] Eleanor Laise, "Best Stock Fund of the Decade: CGM Focus," *The Wall Street Journal*, Dec. 31, 2009, https://www.wsj.com/articles/SB10001424052748704876804574628561609012716.

negative 66.97 percent in 2022.[7] To be clear, we are not criticizing ARK Funds but pointing out how emotions and volatility lead to poor decision-making by the funds' investors.

BUILDING A LEGACY

Amplifying generational stability starts with ensuring spouses work as partners and are both protected in the generation that created or currently controls the wealth. Their period of control can last as long as fifty years.

In cases where a couple is only in their forties and may have sold a business, we have discovered that including any children from the earliest age possible to help them understand the wealth itself helps encourage them to take responsibility and have a vested interest in the success of the family's long-term wealth. Otherwise, there is a high likelihood that the family will experience infighting, greed, confusion, and imbalance.

It is essential that the family members currently controlling the wealth begin this process of educating and involving their children. This can be as simple as giving them stock portfolios to manage. It can be as simple as giving them an allowance but holding them accountable for tracking and spending it. In later stages, it can involve having the children help draft the family constitution and participate in creating and running a family foundation.

---

[7] Amy C. Arnott, "15 Funds That Have Destroyed the Most Wealth over the Past Decade," Morningstar, Feb. 2, 2024, https://www. morningstar.com/funds/15-funds-that-have-destroyed-most-wealth-over-past-decade.

A family foundation is a separate entity that must meet strict legal requirements by having a board, filing annual tax returns, and paying out a percentage of its assets every year to various charities. This structure can offer a great tool to get the children or even grandchildren involved in wealth stewardship and include them in the decision-making, oversight, and management process so that they become emotionally invested in the foundation. It creates objective and tangible results.

This way of building a legacy has become more important to me as I personally witness my own son displaying great personal responsibility, humility, and respect for the wealth his mother and I created. As I see him display these character attributes, I become more motivated to involve him in growing the family wealth, and my personal desire to see him be the beneficiary of that wealth grows.

CHAPTER 6

EXPOSING CLIENT GAPS

In this chapter, I will outline the most common gaps we observe in clients' planning, with the caveat that higher levels of wealth bring more complexity, and we see oversights of all kinds. Part of the utility of a virtual family office is to identify gaps you hadn't even thought of. Here are the top three:

1. The estate plan has been ignored and forgotten, and it hasn't been updated in years. For instance, the beneficiaries haven't been changed. Never mind those pesky new beloved grandchildren! (I kid.)

2. The investments are in no way aligned with the family's current needs, liquidity, tax rates, and so on. We have a tool called Bucketology to address this, which I will talk about in greater detail in the next chapter.
3. Documents regarding business owners, shareholders, partners, and succession are either nonexistent, outdated, or just poorly designed.

In my view, the wealth management industry is to blame for the majority of these gaps, mostly due to its own laziness. Either an advisor was paid an up-front commission long ago and has no incentive to help—for example, just as a realtor who sold your home has no obligation to help you a year after the sale—or they already have your accounts under their management for a fee and are quite comfortable coasting, which they may do until and unless you demand more.

The virtual family office model better addresses these gaps for the following reasons. Number one, it is legally accountable to the client and their family. Number two, we have developed a system we call the Wealth Management Consultative Process, which employs regularly scheduled strategy sessions (typically quarterly) to hold the family accountable and keep the VFO team on top of all issues proactively. Finally, the VFO by definition includes every type of family and wealth planning expert in existence.

UNDERSTANDING BASIC FINANCIAL PRINCIPLES

Another significant gap is in families' understanding of the family office. Its primary function is to educate families on basic financial principles, yet it's surprising how little the wealthy grasp these fundamentals. At a basic level, families in this situation need the solution of getting educated on investing fundamentals. For those of you who may need it, let's do a quick review of the basics first. If you're up to speed, you can skip this section.

Own vs. Loan

A crucial concept when you invest is "own versus loan." On the loan side, various investment avenues exist, including bank accounts, certificates of deposit (CDs), money market funds, corporate bonds, municipal bonds, and fixed immediate insurance products. In these instances, investors essentially lend their capital in exchange for a fixed or guaranteed rate of return, utilizing a straightforward tool to navigate financial decisions.

Historically, the loan return has averaged somewhere between 5 and 6 percent.[8] When you loan money to a company—say, Coca-Cola—it offers to pay you 5 to 6 percent for the use of your money. Now, stop and think for a moment: What must that institution do to pay you a guaranteed 5 to 6 percent rate of return? Well, it's not complicated to figure out. Obviously, the company has to earn a much higher rate of return through its profitability. So, the company needs to earn somewhere north of a 10 to 15 percent rate on its business operations to pay you that fixed return.

---

[8] Roger G. Ibbotson et al., *2019 Stocks, Bonds, Bills, and Inflation (SBBI) Yearbook* (New York: Duff & Phelps, 2018).

On the other side of the ledger, we have what we call "own," which is a type of investing through which you take ownership. These arrangements historically have a much higher rate of return because they are the engine of the American economy and produce profits. Examples would include real estate—a piece of property, commercial or residential, or a real estate investment trust. You could own commodities, like gold, oil, or gas. You could own your own privately held business or own parts of businesses through a private equity fund that owns many other businesses.

You could also own parts of publicly traded companies through stocks. I do not like the word "stock" because it does not do the arrangement justice. In the simplest terms, if you put money in the stock market, you own shares of, say, Coca-Cola. "Stock" literally just comes from the term *stock certificate*, which shows your ownership of a business. When you have a share of stock, you actually have ownership in an ongoing enterprise. I prefer to refer to it as the business market. So if you want to invest in a pool of businesses—say, for example, a fund built of companies in the S&P 500— that would be a form of ownership.

On the ownership side of the ledger, historically the rate of return has been well north of 8 percent and as high as 12 to 15 percent.[9] In publicly traded stocks, when dividends are reinvested, the return has averaged between 10 and 12 percent over the last fifty to one hundred years.[10]

---

[9] Roger G. Ibbotson et al., *2019 Stocks, Bonds, Bills, and Inflation (SBBI) Yearbook* (New York: Duff & Phelps, 2018).
[10] Ibid.

When a family office or any wealth advisor builds a portfolio for a family, they must pair up the possible investment instruments with the family's goals and liquidity needs. The high-level name for this is asset allocation—in other words, how much money needs to be placed in stocks versus bonds versus cash.

Stocks vs. Bonds

It shocks me how many ultra-wealthy business owners don't understand the difference between a stock and a bond of a publicly traded company.

Bond: An investor (that's you) lends money to a company or a government for a set period of time, in exchange for regular interest payments. Once that period of time expires, known as the bond reaching maturity, the bond issuer returns the investor's money.

Stock: A stock represents a share in the ownership of a company, including a claim on the company's earning and assets. As such, stockholders are partial owners of the company.

Let's say you want to invest in a bond—$10,000 to Coca-Cola. The company cannot pay you a guaranteed rate higher than the profit it makes. So, why not buy shares of Coca-Cola stock instead? Stocks historically have a higher rate of return than bonds—roughly a 10 to 12 percent annual return versus about 4 to 6 percent from bonds.[11]

By definition, the bank can't give you higher interest on your deposits than it charges you on a car loan.

---

[11] Roger G. Ibbotson et al., *2019 Stocks, Bonds, Bills, and Inflation (SBBI) Yearbook* (New York: Duff & Phelps, 2018).

That's just basic economics. The shares of a business—whether it's publicly traded or, like mine, privately held—over time will always have a higher rate of return. Otherwise, there would be no lending and no real estate.

Here is a basic way to understand this principle: my office landlord can't charge me more than I make as a percentage profit, or I couldn't afford to be in business. Can you pay more in debt to your banker than you make in profit? Of course not, but the public might be surprised by how few affluent Americans understand this basic concept, and that leads them to "stock-market gambling." The S&P 500 is a list of the five hundred largest publicly traded companies in America. As of this writing, it has more than $1.4 trillion (about $4,500 per person in the U.S.) in cash or dividends and stock buybacks over the past twelve months.[12]

Investing vs. Speculating

Let's examine a fundamental principle: investing versus speculating. I often like to say that there's a fine line between Saturday night and Sunday morning. This little line often rings true: someone might believe they're investing when, in reality, they're speculating. Let me provide an example. Suppose someone sells their business and plans to invest half the profits in cryptocurrency. While cryptocurrency shows promise and potential, it's still in its early stages. It lacks real

---

[12] Bob Carey, "S&P Index Dividends & Stock Buybacks," *Market Commentary Blog*, First Trust Portfolios, July 30, 2024, https://www.ftportfolios.com/blogs/MarketBlog/2024/7/30/sp-500-index-dividends--stock-buybacks.

dividends, generates no income, and doesn't contribute to employment. Moreover, it remains largely untested and unregulated. In contrast, true investments would involve blue-chip stocks or stable real estate holdings. A blue-chip stock refers to the shares of an established, profitable, and well-recognized corporation.

CLIENT ONBOARDING: WEALTH MANAGEMENT CONSULTATIVE PROCESS

Questmont uses a process called the Wealth Management Consultative Process for potential new clients, which begins with a series of three meetings.

The Connection Meeting

When we initially meet with a client, we conduct an hour-long exploratory call and ask very pointed questions to see if we want to take them on as a client and move forward. We ask deep, personal questions about their lifestyle, values, family, religion, and more. If there is an addicted child, we should know that. If there are health issues that would affect the wealth planning, we need to know that. There needs to be a very personal and transparent connection so that we truly know you and how to counsel you. This work is about taking care of and protecting the humans who own the wealth—and providing the best for them. Wealth is merely the toolbox with which to implement that care and protection.

Wealth Management Consultative Process

THE CONNECTION MEETING

In-depth understanding of your values, family, objectives, income, assets, etc.

THE INVESTMENT CONSULTATION MEETING

- Analysis and gaps presented
- Stress test completed
- Recommendations for moving forward and how to maximize the value of your life's work

THE ENGAGEMENT MEETING

- Paperwork signed to initiate your plan
- Priorities set

THE LAUNCH MEETING

Orientation into the Questmont Experience

THE STRATEGY SESSIONS

- Ongoing progress and strategizing
- Implementation of future strategy sessions

Questmont
VIRTUAL FAMILY OFFICE

- The VFO is a best-in-class team of experts, each with a high level of knowledge and skill in key financial areas.
- Our VFO team will be brought in to evaluate and create a 360° review of your financial situation and devise appropriate solutions.

Part of the deep connection and discovery meeting is identifying your high-net-worth personality, as outlined in Chapter 4. At our firm, we have identified the characteristics of our families. They tend to be more independent and libertarian, with a "live and let live" mentality, and they are very family-oriented. They have a powerful work ethic and are entrepreneurial. They tend to live below their means. They place a high value on the concept of having a personal CFO and trusted advisory team to lead them, advise them, and defend them. They also place an extremely high value on honesty and independence. They possess some other traits, such as being a first-generation business owner, very conscientious, and driven. They prefer their advisors to function as genuine advocates on their behalf.

Does your team know you this well?

We also talk to new clients about their current advisors. Do they have lawyers? An accountant? Property and casualty insurance or commercial insurance advisors? Do they have wealth managers or financial advisors? If so, who are they? We uncover how often they meet with these advisors, how often they have changed advisors, and their satisfaction level with their advisors.

Wealth Stress Test

Following this connection process, we prepare diagnostics and run a wealth stress test to verify that all of the current plans and strategies are optimally aligned to meet your dreams, goals, and objectives. This test analyzes the five areas where there might be gaps:

1. Investing as it relates to your goals
2. Asset protection and insurance

3. Business analytics for business owners
4. Estate planning for efficient tax mitigation and getting money to heirs
5. Efficiently optimizing your charitable intent

We have discovered some very substantial gaps when putting our clients through the wealth stress test.* One couple sold their commercial air-conditioning business and hired an advisor, whom they had known for twenty years. First, we know from experience that hiring a friend isn't always the best option for your wealth management needs. Second, in this case, he was essentially a commission-based advisor with a self-interest in selling particular funds. Through the process of working on the stress test together, we discovered the client was overpaying by $66,000 a year in fees and taxes. By reallocating their funds into lower-cost options and implementing more tax-efficient strategies, we were able to save them $72,000 per year. Simply by identifying this overpayment and restructuring their funds, we were able to recoup some of that money for them, giving them a $6,000-per-month raise.

In another scenario, a client wanted to sell a medical business. More than thirty years prior, he had very lovingly set up a pension plan—not a 401(k)—for his employees. He made contributions on their behalf but, through ignorance, accidentally titled all of those accounts at the local bank in his personal name. This created a terrible problem for the buyer of the business because they would be taking on massive legal liability. We had to come up with a solution: either beg the IRS for forgiveness and simply retire the accounts, or close out the pension plan and generously roll over all the lump sums to the employees, giving them the money that had been protected for forty years.

Someone else had a life insurance policy with a $10 million death benefit. They'd been divorced for several years, but their ex-husband was still the beneficiary, and the wealth advisor whom they were paying $150,000 a year never discovered this issue. We also discovered that they had a shortage of current income to fund their lifestyle, but there was $2.5 million of cash value in that insurance policy, which could easily be used to generate an additional $150,000 of income per year. Tapping into that resource solved a big gap in that client's income plan.

In another case, a business owner had $11 million in the company's 401(k) plan, for which he was the sponsor and trustee. He had worked with his "trusted advisor." Through the wealth stress test, we discovered that the advisor was charging an extra fee of 1 percent a year above the national average. Simply by getting the 401(k) fee benchmarked to where it ought to be, we saved him over $110,000 a year, and that was seven years ago. It's now over $500,000 a year in savings, which he has passed on to his employees.

For the two or three decades that we have been offering these wealth stress tests, 100 percent of the individuals and families who've gone through this process have benefited from it, agree with it, and love it. Over 70 percent of the families that go through this process retain us. In some cases, at the end of that process, we discover they are not a good fit, usually because of their high-net-worth personality as it relates to receiving and following financial advice.

PROTECTING WEALTH IN THE GOLDEN YEARS

Recently, a client made two mistakes: one was speculating rather than investing, which then created a large gap in his wealth plan*. He was a retired surgeon, over eighty years old with $10 million of investments, 100 percent of which was in two small upstart technology stocks. He also needed to pull out about $700,000 a year to satisfy his required minimum distribution (RMD), which he needed to live on, fund his family's lifestyle, and donate to the cancer charities that they were so passionate about.

RMD: REQUIRED MINIMUM DISTRIBUTION

Upon turning seventy-three years old, every American has to pull money out of their traditional 401(k)s and IRAs. The RMD is a percentage of the total account value that increases as you age. Think of your own savings. If you have a traditional IRA, you're not paying tax on that now. You're going to pay tax in the future, when you make withdrawals (distributions). At age seventy-three, the IRS forces you to start withdrawing. The first year, that RMD is 3.65 percent. Let's say you have $1 million in your traditional IRA; when you turn seventy-three, you have to take out $36,500. By the time you're eighty, that percentage goes up to 7 percent. The IRS wants you to withdraw the money (ergo, pay your taxes) before you die.

When we did the gap analysis for the retired surgeon, we learned that his wife was very scared that her husband had become obsessed with these two stocks, which in one year had fallen 70 percent. We completed a life optimization chart (which I'll talk about in Chapter 7), and because one of his goals was to leave each of his children and grandchildren at least $1 million, we were able to conclude that he needed to diversify $6.5 million of the $10 million into a more durable portfolio. Through the life optimization chart, the wealth stress test, and the gap analysis, we were able to give this client very specific numbers on how much he needed to diversify out of those two highly speculative stocks.

Now, let me hammer the crap out of the financial advice industry—because for the previous thirty years, that $10 million had been invested with three of the "Big Four" financial institutions. All three of them tried desperately to persuade this client to diversify some of that money because they were not able to charge him any fees or commissions when it was dormant in two stocks. So, their "advice" was a feeble attempt to try to make themselves money. However, they never gave him a compelling, fact-based guideline for how much he needed to diversify in order to protect his wife, be protective of his children and grandchildren, and protect the charities he's so passionate about.

One of the gaps we routinely discover when onboarding a new family is their lack of a process and lack of a coordinated team. Often, no one has asked basic questions such as "How often does your team of advisors get together specifically to work on your wealth plan?" and "How often does your wealth advisor review your tax return?"

As you can see, the potential gaps come in many flavors, sizes, and colors. In all of these instances, clients had preexisting advisors, CPAs, and attorneys, but none of them caught the gaps. Worse still, in some cases *they created the problems.*

The Investment Consultation Meeting

To analyze and address gaps, we also conduct an investment consultation, usually two to four weeks after the connection meeting. We share all the gaps we identified—and there are often many, some of which are substantial and will hurt the clients or their families. Through these consultations, we have discovered issues such as a business where the majority owner had three different formulas for partners who had just been brought on versus partners he was buying out. This situation virtually guaranteed he would get sued.

We also give them diagnostics that we have done the analytics for and provide fairly pointed, specific ideas for solutions that they could and should implement. At this stage, we give them very specific action, such as an estate plan, a tax plan, a plan for portfolio reallocation, an exit strategy, and anything else they might need.

Engagement Meeting

After we have done the wealth stress test and all parties have confirmed that we want to work together, we agree to the pricing and call an engagement meeting, typically thirty to forty-five days later. This is where all of the documents are signed, and any liquid assets are transferred. In our case, we have high minimums, requiring at least 50 percent of the client's liquid assets or our minimum—whichever is greater—to be under our care.

The Launch Meeting

From there, we focus on orientation into the Questmont experience and identify the next planning steps. As I've written before, inertia can be dangerous, insidious, and easy to ignore. Not taking action can sometimes be as problematic as doing the wrong thing. That's why taking action is part of the Wealth Management Consultative Process. We use a tool called an Advanced Planning Mind Map, which lists all the actions needed to optimize the plan. I'll describe this tool in more detail later in the next chapter.

The Strategy Sessions

Once you've identified the gaps, it is essential to put a process in place to fix them. It is virtually impossible for an ultra-high-net-worth family with complex financial situations to fully repair these gaps immediately, and a proven, airtight process is essential. To achieve this, we conduct strategy sessions on a regular, preset basis. I'll describe them in more detail in the next chapter.

The Lifelong Journey

The second part of the Wealth Management Consultative Process is a one-page document called the Lifelong Journey. Together with the Advanced Planning Mind

Map, these two documents illustrate the backbone of how we deliver a wealth plan. These tools remove the fear and uncertainty while mitigating risk. Clients enter into an ongoing consultative relationship.

Wealth management is a process. It's not a one-off. It's for life. And done properly, it is multigenerational. Once a family has retained us, we walk them through our process. Through this planning and accountability structure, we ensure that our clients overcome their inertia, address their gaps head-on, and can start optimizing their investments and their lives.

The Lifelong Journey

TAX PLANNING

I. Basics
1. Maximize deductions
2. Minimize dividends, income, taxable gains

II. Sophisticated
1. Captive insurance
2. Defined benefit pensions / deferred comp
3. Section 1202 and 1042 planning
4. Cost segregation / accelerated depreciation

ESTATE/ CHARITABLE

I. Basics
Wills / testamentary trusts / POAs

II. Complex
Intentionally defective grantor trusts, generation-skipping trusts, ILITs

III. Kindhearted
Charitable trusts, family foundations, donor-advised funds

BUSINESS ANALYTICS

I. Basics
Buy/sell, company-sponsored retirement plan, entity structure

II. Advanced
1. Succession plans (sell, ESOP, PE, internal)
2. Capital structure and reorganization

ASSET PROTECTION / INSURANCE PLANNING

I. Protector
1. Basic life insurance
2. Basic disability insurance
3. Long-term care insurance

II. Evolved
1. Irrevocable life insurance trusts
2. Buy/sell life and disability to cover your business
3. Private placement life insurance
4. Captive insurance company
5. Entity creation, asset structure
6. Creating anonymity

INVESTMENT CONSULTING

I. Basics
1. Asset allocation
2. Behavioral investment counseling
3. Tax management
4. Security-backed line of credit

II. Graduate
1. Due diligence on private investments and pet projects
2. Hedge funds / reorganization strategies

CHAPTER 7

TAKE OFF THE BLINDERS

At Questmont, we have a host of tools to help clients optimize their businesses, their wealth, and, by extension, their lives. The more you know about the process, the better positioned you'll be to make the most of your opportunities.

THE PHASES OF A BUSINESS EXIT

When business owners go through an exit, sale, or retirement, they often face a range of complex emotional challenges. As specialists working with business owners during these transitions, we've identified four key phases that many experience.

Phase 1: Retiring

The business owner may feel a sense of freedom and possibility. This is the phase that most people have in mind when they picture their ideal retirement: *Take a big vacation. Have fun in the sun all day. I can do what I want. There is no alarm clock.*

Phase 2: Feeling Loss and Lost

The second phase typically begins to set in about a year after retirement. The business owner begins to ask questions like "Is that all there is?" They have lost their old orientation to the big five: routines, identity, purpose, relationships, and power. This period is particularly painful and difficult since so many changes happen at once. We start to see the "3Ds": divorce, depression, and decline. Many feel fear and anxiety, and most begin to work on those feelings.

Phase 3: Using Trial and Error

The retiree experiments with new hobbies, causes, or ways to find meaning. This can be a difficult but important step towards the final phase. There will be some strikeouts—some attempts at hobbies, charities, or finding purpose will fail. The question to ask at this phase is "How can I make my life meaningful again and contribute?" It is important to keep trying and experimenting.

Phase 4: Rewiring and Reinventing

Retirees can recover from all five losses and find a new sense of routine, identity, relationships, purpose, and personal power. This process almost always involves some form of helping others.

Understanding and preparing for these emotional stages can help business owners navigate this major life transition more smoothly.

THE QUESTMONT INVESTMENT PROCESS

A client's portfolio can't be built until after their plan is done. Through the Questmont Wealth Management Consultative Process, we connect their plan to the investment strategy. There are three main components to the Questmont investment process: life optimization chart, Bucketology, and asset allocation.

Step 1: Life Optimization Chart

We work with the family to develop the overall wealth plan using our life optimization chart, a simple tool that we named but was put in front of me by a big investment firm twenty years ago. We break down a family's goals, objectives, and needs into four quadrants:

1. Things they want to do now
2. Things they want to do later
3. Things they must do now
4. Things they must do later

We have the family fill out the chart twice. First, they complete it based on their current wants and understanding of their situation.

Post-Stress-Test Life Optimization Chart

Initial Client Answers

Want to Now

- Purchase $1,900,000 beach house
- Give $90,000/year to charity that helps the homeless
- Give $90,000/year to their church
- Sell business

Want to Later

- Purchase $900,000 yacht

Have to Now

- Prep the business for sale
- Maintain lifestyle at $900,000 annually

Have to Later

- Fund college for both children
  - $150,000 + inflation
  - Start year will be 2034
- $900,000 income for life

Once we've met with the family and determined the objectives—whether they be donating to charity, buying a jet or beach house, or funding children's college tuition—we assign each one to the appropriate quadrant and calculate the approximate cost now and in the future. This exercise provides a picture of the family's short-term and long-term liquidity and cash flow needs.

Whether you're a millionaire, a pentamillionaire, or a decamillionaire, you don't have enough wealth to do everything on the planet. You must make tough decisions about how to allocate your capital, time, and resources. Our process helps clients make informed and empowered decisions regarding what they can afford to allocate capital toward.

We have a software program that helps us first determine whether clients have enough wealth to cover their have-tos. This is a stress test that sorts needs from desires. Sometimes when we run the numbers, they don't work. For instance, if the family buys a yacht, they won't be able to afford their kids' college education; or if the yacht's too big, it might hurt their retirement income goal later. If the client is willing to change some of the goals and reduce certain expenditures to support higher priorities, we can give them a picture of what's possible without dinging their wealth.

Based on the stress test and related discussion about priorities, we then collaboratively update the chart with needs and wants based on the concrete numbers.

Then, we execute on this plan and fund all four quadrants of their goals as they laid them out in the Questmont life optimization chart.

Post-Stress-Test Life Optimization Chart

Revised in Consultation with Wealth Manager

Want to Now

- Purchase $1,700,000 beach house
- Give $80,000/year to charity that helps the homeless
- Give $80,000/year to their church
- Sell business

Want to Later

- Purchase $800,000 yacht

Have to Now

- Prep the business for sale
- Maintain lifestyle at $900,000 annually

Have to Later

- Fund college for both children
  - $150,000 + inflation
  - Start year will be 2034
- $900,000 income for life

THE DREAMS-TO-GROUNDING RATIO

There is a common mistake that people make, particularly after a liquidity event such as a business sale or a divorce. Our chief of staff identified this problem and named it the "dreams-to-grounding ratio." In other words, though they have substantial assets, their eyes are even bigger than their wallets. We can cite many instances where families begin making poor decisions following an exit event.

For instance, we assisted a business owner in their late forties with selling their business to a private equity fund, buying out their partner, and remaining as CEO.* They engaged our services prior to the sale, while being advised by a law firm that aimed to establish a set of entities for a significant fee.

Upon conducting a wealth stress test with our valuation and entity experts, we discovered the lawyers' plan to allocate half of the business proceeds into charitable remainder trusts. This allocation would have undermined the family's wealth objectives, such as purchasing a yacht and a beach condo as well as educating their children. It was clearly a strategy to take advantage of the client's desire to mitigate taxes during the sale of the business and prey on that fear.

The family, however, was not ready to prioritize substantial charitable giving, and the proposed structure would have required literally giving away a huge percentage of their newfound wealth. So, after we defended them and set them on a path to make wise decisions with their capital, we observed that their dreams-to-grounding ratio went crazy. Though we helped them see how to fund multiple major dreams, they went after objectives that contradicted their stated priorities.

We had utilized the life optimization tool to determine that they could meet their annual income goal of $1 million and were able to fully fund college tuition for both of their children, give annual gifts to their church, and afford a beach condo. However, surprisingly, they immediately shifted gears and purchased a yacht for twice the price that we had built into the plan. Not long after, they bought a beach property for double the amount we'd allocated. These choices had the net effect of increasing their annual cost of living due to the maintenance costs while also decreasing the amount of income coming to the family as the investment pool shrank. We can give the best advice based on the most comprehensive data, but it will only benefit people if they listen.

Step 2: Bucketology

Once we've conducted the wealth stress test and filled out the life optimization chart, we compare this analysis with the client's current asset structure. We call this process Bucketology. We developed the Bucketology tool to help simplify and teach clients the four types of money and wealth:

Bucket 1: Cash. This includes money in bank accounts, certificates of deposit, and U.S. government bonds.

Bucket 2: After-Tax Accounts. This is money invested after taxes, also known as nonqualified investments. Such investments include stocks, bonds, REITs, and commodities.

Bucket 3: Pre-Tax Accounts. These are qualified investments that are usually publicly traded. They include

Bucketology

pensions, 401(k)s, and IRAs. Assets that have been invested on a pre-tax basis will be taxed at withdrawal or death.

Bucket 4: Illiquid Wealth. This category includes real estate holdings, hedge funds, and ownership of private companies. For many business owners, illiquid wealth is tied up in the family business. Since the shares of my company, Questmont, represent the largest part of my net worth, I have a lot of illiquid wealth. Often, business owners own warehouses or the offices where their businesses are housed. They may own other investment and rental properties as well, both commercial and residential. And finally, there are private equity funds. Venture capital funds and hedge funds fall into this fourth bucket due to their long-term nature, volatility, and illiquidity.

ALIGNING LIQUIDITY AND FINANCIAL GOALS

We then take the Bucketology continuum and try to match it up with the four quadrants of goals that the client has identified, to see if they work together. We're trying to determine the cash flow of the family and make sure that they have an adequate balance of those four buckets to protect them.

For instance, one client had to sell his business because the family had borrowed too much.* The bank told him he was way over the covenants—the agreements he'd made with the institution—and the only way he could raise enough capital was to sell. He wasn't actually in that much debt; he'd just broken the rules of the loan.

Another way of thinking about this step is to ask: Are these investments creating enough cash flow and liquidity to meet the goals on the desired timeline? For example, if a client wanted to purchase a vacation home in three years, what would the source of the funds be? This category also covers any insurance that they have in place.

Step 3: Asset Allocation

Once we've developed a life optimization plan and looked at the Bucketology, that information informs how we allocate assets into the nonqualified and qualified buckets.

For nonqualified accounts, we have to take the client's tax bracket into consideration, so we're using tax management strategies. This could mean buying individual securities rather than passive funds, in order to manage the resulting tax issues. By buying the individual security, a client can minimize their tax hit. For example, if the overall stock market is up one day, but one hundred stocks are down, we can tax-loss harvest by selling some of those individual securities.

We have a money manager who looks at those opportunities on a daily basis, so we're able to do tax-loss selling daily. This strategy adds considerable return to the client because they're able to use the losses over time to offset the profits that they will inevitably have.

Different goals often have different asset allocations because they may have different time horizons. One goal may be thirty years out, while another is only seven years. These two goals clearly should have different asset allocations and different structures.

Over twenty years ago, we began partnering with a $1.5 trillion trust company. It helps us act as an outsourced chief investment officer so that we don't have to push our own funds. It identifies and vets 140 of the best money managers on the planet, allowing us to choose the absolute top managers to make the day-to-day decisions on our clients' behalf. On any given day, we have 140 of the best money managers managing assets and an additional 140 on the bench. We keep them on a thirty-day rolling contract, so if they underperform or if top people retire, we are able to push them out. We go in and look at the portfolio on a quarterly basis to see if we need to rebalance among the asset classes. Because we don't have any money managers on staff, there is no self-dealing and no conflict of interest.

Nobel Prize–winning economist Harry Markowitz conducted a study that concluded asset allocation is the largest determinant of portfolio returns and risk.[13] Allocation will determine over 90 percent of your portfolio's success over time. Other factors like security selection (a fancy way of saying which stock or bond you choose) and market timing (when you get in or out of the market or a particular investment) only determine approximately 10 percent.

Let me illustrate this principle. Let's say you went to Questmont, Fidelity, Vanguard, and Merrill Lynch and you gave us each an equal amount of money and the same asset allocation request, such as 10 percent in foreign stocks, 20 percent in real estate investment trusts, and so on. Over time, every company's portfolio would

---

[13] Ann Behan, "Harry Markowitz: Creator of Modern Portfolio Theory," *Investopedia*, Aug. 2, 2024, https://www.investopedia.com/terms/h/harrymarkowitz.asp.

look remarkably similar because each of the funds we chose would be the same. How you allocate your money in the first place is the biggest determining factor of your results.

My industry doesn't really want you to know that fact, because security selection and market timing are based more on fear and greed—buy, sell, buy, sell—and that activity is where they make money on the trades. When the stock market drops 3 percent in one day, my industry generally likes that. A broker can call and say, "Let's get out of this" or "Let's buy a bond," and either the institution or the advisor can make more money. Even if they aren't making more money, it makes them feel more relevant. The two factors that account for 10 percent of the success do matter, but they're not the big kahuna. The big kahuna is nailing that allocation.

QUARTERLY REBALANCING

Finally, we go in and look at the portfolio on a quarterly basis to see if we need to rebalance among the asset classes.

What we do is really kind of boring. We execute an extremely well-thought-out, detailed wealth plan, and then we build your allocation. Every time you go to change it, know what we do? We tell you to stop it. *Stop that!* We only change it if there is a significant change in income, such as an inheritance, a business sale, or a lottery win. This goes back to first principles: it's the planning, stupid.

I bring this up as a basic tutorial but also as a warning: the financial advice industry will make more money if you are scared or believe that jumping in and out of the market or individual stocks represents the ultimate path to success. In fact, building a portfolio that has the appropriate asset allocation for your specific goals is most important and will often involve less activity in your portfolio, thereby making the financial advisor and the financial advisor's firm less money and causing them to feel less important.

MORE OPTIONS IN THE TOOLBOX

There are two other tools that are important to discuss: the Total Client Profile and the Advanced Planning Mind Map, which we share with clients at the investment consultation meeting.

The Total Client Profile

There are seven key categories that we cover and get to know in detail about our families:

1. **Values.** We start with a deep, deep dive into understanding their values around money, love, charity, politics, religion, and other core issues. In particular, we have a series of embedded questions from a psychologist to try to understand their values around money.
2. **Goals.** We examine their goals and often discover they haven't been clearly defined. We help facilitate the client in uncovering their desires and dreams, as well as attaching specific dollar amounts to each goal. Those goals inform the four quadrants of the life optimization chart I described.

Total Client Profile Mind Map

3. **Relationships.** Who are the most important people in their lives? This could be their children, spouses, business partners, employees, advisors, friends, neighbors, and fellow church members.
4. **Assets and Liabilities.** We then look at their assets, both liquid and illiquid, as well as their income sources.
5. **Process.** It's important for my team to know how each client likes to interact with their professionals. How involved do they like to be in the management of their finances? Do they prefer written or electronic communications? Who else do they want involved in the process? We also inquire about their confidentiality needs. The wealthier families get more security and privacy regarding intimate matters because they become targets of unscrupulous people.
6. **Interests.** We review their interests, including hobbies, dream vacations, donating time to church or charities, spending time with family, international travel, and any other key interests they have.
7. **Advisors.** We identify their current CPA, lawyer, insurance agent, and financial advisors.

We then put the information gathered on these categories into a one-page visual chart called a Total Client Profile. One of the benefits of this chart is that it can be easily communicated and shared with other advisors like attorneys, CPAs, their CFOs, and children and grandchildren.

Advanced Planning Mind Map

Ultra-high-net-worth families tend to have very complex situations. The mind map we provide clients is

Advanced Planning Tracker

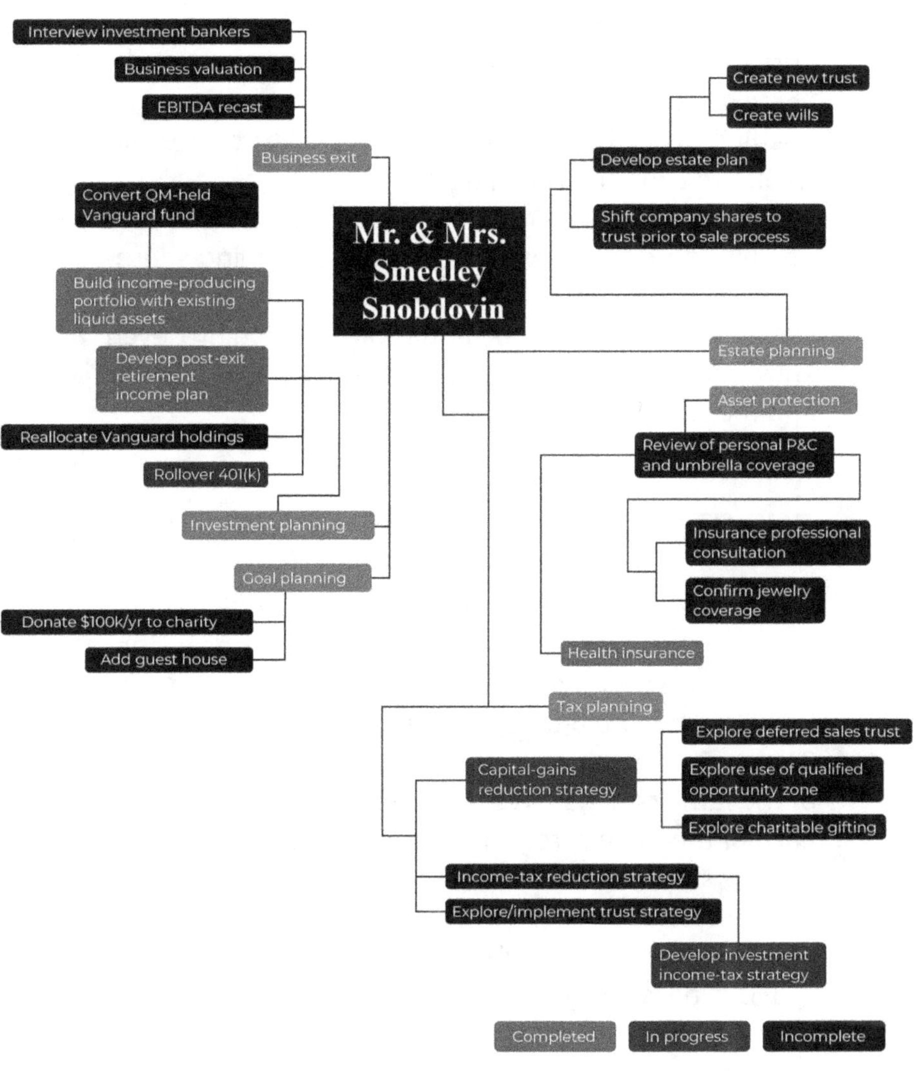

color coded like a stoplight: every item is highlighted in green, yellow, or red to signify whether a) we have completed the planning task, b) it is in process, or c) we haven't touched it yet. This tool is a simple, colorful way for the family to track all their initiatives, responsibilities, and assets—and ultimately lessen the complexity.

We go through an in-depth process to help our clients identify their important goals in each category. For example, "have to" now could be as simple as needing to pay bills, "have to" later could be dispersing wealth to continue their lifestyle.

With the right leadership and guidance, clients should be able to rid themselves of the overwhelming sensations they feel, optimize their finances, maximize the value of their businesses, find money they didn't even know they had, quit operating from a place of scarcity, and focus on their families.

THE STRATEGY SESSIONS

This process is simply a series of prescheduled meetings, often quarterly, with a linear progression. Preschedules are one of the best tools that we've ever built. We may hold these strategy sessions as often as five or six times a year, depending on the complexity of the family's needs. We have developed a checklist in each of the main categories for each meeting:

1. Tax planning
2. Estate and charitable planning
3. Business analytics
4. Asset protection
5. Investment consulting

This structure ensures everyone addresses the most pressing issues on a regular basis and ensures that nothing gets forgotten or swept under the rug. It effectively forces us to conduct a mini wealth stress test every time we meet the family so that their wealth is optimized, their strategies are cutting-edge, and nothing falls off the table.

We do wealth management, actually delivered, meaning we help you strategize *and then implement the strategy*. This is the process that brings the magic to life, because we keep steering your boat down the stream. But if you get out of the river, we can't help you.

It is the family office's job (or wealth advisor's role) to act as "a dashboard" at each one of these meetings to highlight and bring to attention the most urgent gaps.

For example, if the estate plan is out of date, that might be the highest priority, in which case the best attorneys and estate-planning experts would be called to attend that meeting to specifically address that piece of the plan. In another scenario, a business owner might be ready to sell or exit. In that case, business analytics would be at the meeting, and we might hold future meetings to evaluate the business and come up with a plan that complements the owner's personality. We'll help the owner choose the proper exit strategy, whether it's a sale through an investment banker, a sale to a competitor, an employee stock ownership plan (ESOP), a management buyout, or another available option.

The strategy sessions fix existing gaps and, by being proactive, prevent new ones from arising. These meetings address the client's needs and remove the complexities, unburdening the family and allowing them to move on to productive pursuits. They might use their newfound time to firmly establish a legacy, such as through a family constitution, foundation, or simple donor-advised fund.

Furthermore, having these regular strategy sessions allows them to conduct a wealth stress test. Many billionaires use these wealth stress tests on an ongoing basis to ensure that their current strategies and plans will optimally achieve the outcomes and goals that they desire, now and in the future.

In other words, we know what we're doing. It's very deliberate. And we're going to have regularly scheduled sessions to triage whichever areas need the most attention.

ENVISIONING NEW PATHS

When a prospective family is onboarding, we explain that our strategy sessions are going to cover the human side of whatever's happening in their lives, and in addition, we're going to pull in experts to cover each specific area of need. Wealthy families need and deserve leadership.

They also often need encouragement to envision new paths that they couldn't even have imagined for themselves. The second part of our wealth management process is the exciting part of the work. It's where we take the culmination of wealth, facts, and minutiae and start showing the family what they can do with their wealth—how much they can afford to give to their church, how much they can afford to give to charity, and what lifestyle they can afford. Is it a new boat? Is it a new home? Is it gifts for the grandchildren? The problem with "envisioning new paths" is that most of the time, no one has ever sat down and explained to the family that the dreams they have for their wealth first need to be categorized. Once they see those laid out in the life optimization chart, they are able to picture what's truly possible for their future.

Their wealth, effort, and lifetime of work have afforded them the ability to pursue bigger dreams, but often no one has pointed out what's possible. This is a huge gap in the wealth management and financial advice industry. We like to say leadership transforms and advice informs. Obviously they need advice, but they need empowerment to transform as well. A good advisor will give them all the right tools and strongly encourage them to follow the plan that the family office believes is in the client's ultimate best interest. They need full confidence that their team has the necessary wisdom, knowledge, experience, and competency to maximize their outcomes.

This is only my opinion, but it's based on nearly four decades of grinding: a miniscule percentage of financial advisors can actually deliver this high level of service, particularly with regard to business exits. Most are simply unable, because often, if they work for a large firm, they haven't experienced these entrepreneurial milestones themselves.

Not Just about the Money

My mission has long been to assemble the necessary tools and processes to best serve highly financially successful families and truly represent and defend them, without giving in to the temptations of the financial advice industry. I could have taken the easier path in exchange for selfish financial benefits, but not only would it have created a conflict of interest, it would have meant selling my soul. My approach is to give wealthy families a different perspective and a second opinion. I have yet to see other firms use an independent consultative process like ours, which is really a way of advising and leading a family over their entire lifetime.

CHAPTER 8

SELECTING THE RIGHT FINANCIAL ADVISOR: DO THEY DEFEND AND DELIGHT?

How do you select the right financial advisor? First, find the largest dead cat, with the longest tail you can find, and begin swinging it as fast as you can. Period. My grandmother used to say, "You can't swing a dead cat without hitting an insurance salesman or an attorney." It was meant to be derogatory, and I have simply modernized it to include wealth advisors. You can exclude any financial advisors that are hit by the cat from your search, because there are too many of them.

GAPS BETWEEN INVESTORS AND ADVISORS DISAPPOINT

Any version of a family office or other high-level wealth management experience always starts and ends with the human element. As I described in Chapter 3, to keep our team on the forefront of innovation and ensure we understand our clients and prospective families, we underwrite in-depth research to understand wealthy families and their needs, regularly conduct interviews with business owners who have exited or will be exiting, and talk to ultra-affluent families who already have liquidity. We use this research to continually develop and improve our tools, methodologies, and strategies, thus optimizing our services for the families we touch.

As the heat map from the introduction demonstrates, we have discovered there is a yawning gap in the industry between what clients need and what advisors deliver. It stands to reason that advisors should align their services with the benefits affluent clients want to receive, but our research indicates that investors and advisors are currently not on the same page—most investors do not believe they're receiving the right services for a good value. Investor attitudes also vary by net worth, adding another layer of complexity.

When we interviewed wealthy families, 29 percent reported being concerned about leaving a legacy for their heirs. However, advisors thought that this was a 61 percent concern. Taking care of their parents, meanwhile, scored 25.6 percent, but advisors scored it at 56 percent. Twenty-five percent of wealthy families reported that taking care of their pets in the estate plan in the event of an accident or death was important to them, but 0 percent of advisors were asking them about it. Eighty-nine percent of wealthy families want tax planning, yet only 24.8 percent receive it from their advisors. Given what I know about the industry, these numbers are not surprising, but they disgust me.

Clearly, advisors aren't listening to their clients. If you have a pet, imagine how you would feel if you and your spouse died and you had no care plan in place. What would happen to your pet? Most wealth managers don't give this issue any thought. At my firm, we use our research to fix these kinds of gaps for clients. We can include the pets in the estate plan or even create trusts for them.

When my practice was based in Harrisburg, Pennsylvania, we had a partnership with the Pennsylvania Medical Society and the Hershey Medical Center. We provided educational workshops for new doctors, which led to many surgeons and medical specialists hiring my firm. As a result, we decided to do a deeper dive and interview them individually to better understand their needs and desires. We interviewed one hundred surgeons. In exchange for an hour of their time with the researchers, we'd make a donation to their favorite charity.

Very carefully, we developed one hundred questions to get to know ultra-high-net-worth clients better. The process took over a year, but we learned quite a bit. For example, we mistakenly thought that liability or lawsuits—things like asset protection—would be their number one concern, but it was not. The state of Pennsylvania had recently made some legal changes that made it harder for doctors to get sued and limited their exposure. We eventually published the research in a white paper and shared it with all the subjects who participated as well as our entire team, so we all understood this demographic extremely well.

Part of the differentiator in working with Questmont rather than other financial firms is our clients get the expertise that comes from participation in a legitimate wealth management family office mastermind group. Very few of my competitors in the industry can claim that. The mastermind directly benefits our clients because part of our fee pays for its in-depth research on wealthy families and their advisors.

Provocative Questions

Our consultants developed a series of provocative questions designed to uncover whether respondents' current advisors knew them deeply and were delivering a world-class wealth management experience:

1. How well do your current professionals, such as accountants and financial advisors, truly understand you as a person, and not just your financial situation?
2. How often do your professionals work with the top specialists in fields beyond their own expertise to deliver you the best available solutions?
3. How often do your professionals help you "jump the line" when it comes to getting the solutions you need?

4. Do your professionals provide or have access to the deepest expertise and very best solutions available?
5. Do your professionals use a systematic process to catch and correct any failures and to monitor your situation on an ongoing basis to help ensure that your financial and related situations are being effectively managed?
6. Do your professionals evaluate your solutions to determine whether you're on the best possible course or whether an alternative would be more appropriate or effective?

Take the time now to ask yourself these six questions. Answered honestly, they will reveal your current situation. Maybe you are in great financial shape—or assessing your current advisor, you may realize, *Holy crap! I'm in trouble.*

We routinely encounter wealthy people who are being advised by a family member or a friend they have known for ten or twenty years. We like to joke that it's often their golf buddy. When we survey them, they often share that they know deep down that they've outgrown these advisors, yet they simply have not done the work to find new ones. It is because the pain isn't high enough for them to change.

Many challenges come with successfully optimizing a wealthy family's life—and yes, I do say optimizing their lives, not just their wealth. Inertia is the biggest factor that keeps the wealthy from taking action to optimize their lives and, in some cases, the lives of their families and their employees. It holds them back from providing more charitable funding, from paying less to the government, and from having more generational stability.

Here's an example. We frequently host parties and experiences for our clients. At one event, an investment banker—let's call him Carl—was selling a business for $150 million. He brought one of the minority partners, Ryan, to the party, because he thought Ryan would be a lead for us. Ryan was poised to exit the business with around $20 million and would need help managing that wealth. The majority owner that he worked with had been in a group with me for two years, so I knew who was managing their wealth, and I knew they were getting absolutely terrible service.

That was three years ago. Carl was about to experience one of the biggest professional events of his life. The least he should have done was to get a second opinion by going through our process. It would have taken four hours of his life. Worst case, the information would help hold the existing advisors to account and confirm whether the deal was already in good hands. But he just brushed it off.

There is always something—some gap, some tax bill, some legal issue, some additional liquidity—that pays for the four hours tenfold. That's a fact. The problem is many people don't perceive me as being different enough. They think we provide the same service as everyone else. This kind of complacency, dismissiveness, or plain inertia is what frustrates me the most. In the following pages, I'll give you some tips for ensuring you don't let inertia derail you from reaching the highest potential of your wealth.

BEGIN INTERVIEWING ADVISORS

We have a motto in my family and at my firm: "If it is worth doing, it is worth doing well." Here are some best practices for finding the right advisor for you.

You need to be exceptionally selective and more stringent than most wealthy Americans. So maybe you already have a CERTIFIED FINANCIAL PLANNER® professional (CFP®) and a CPA. Those are smart people to have, but that's table stakes.

You want to hire someone with the right credentials, while taking the extra step of asking your potential advisor some basic questions to understand their motives and incentives. For instance:

1. **Do they have a quota? Do they receive sales rewards?** When a client hires a wealth manager, there's an assumption it will be a lifelong relationship. However, quotas mean the advisor has to sell, which implies they must move on. That dynamic diminishes or completely crushes the advisor's ability to take on clients. You're a transaction to them. I don't have a sales reward. I'm self-employed. No one's sending me on a cruise. Can you see how the mindsets are radically different?
2. **Are they employed by an insurance company or brokerage?** If so, they represent the insurance company or brokerage, not you.
3. **Do they have their own funds?** For example, a financial advisor working at a large brokerage may sell you funds that have lower performance, are self-dealing, and have higher fees. They do better for their own firm than they do for clients.

Ask about Their Process

I would ask a great deal about their process as well. Start with these:

1. **What is their investment process?**
2. **More importantly, what is their planning process?** This goes back to "It's the planning, stupid—not just the investing." Quite frankly, investing has become more of a commodity. It is now less expensive on many "do it yourself" platforms.

As I described in Chapter 7, asset allocation is the biggest determiner of investment results—90 percent of the equation. That's a fact my industry doesn't want you to know.

How we differentiate is a small piece in the investment space. So if I'm going to charge you a fee to do that, what else do I offer you? I better do that piece really well, because I'm going to look pretty similar to the other investment banks. This is where the planning, high-touch service, and consulting come in.

In order to differentiate themselves, true wealth managers must offer valuable planning services at no extra charge. Are they actually offering other wealth management services, such as behavioral investment counseling, business consulting, and tax planning?

Let's say two of the Big Four and I all built the same asset allocation, but one of us has a heavy emphasis on lifeboat drills—my firm calls it behavioral investment counseling. When the market went down 57 percent in 2008 to 2009, it was broadly considered the worst recession since the Great Depression. I believe my clients fared better because we didn't allow them to panic and sell. Most Americans underperform their own funds, but I try to position my clients so they don't.

In other words, even though we three advisors might build the same model to start, if we don't all hold the clients' feet to the fire, we'll have different returns in the end. Behavioral investment counseling is building a portfolio based on the wealth plan—and then *sticking to that portfolio*. We don't let emotions override the plan.

Do They Need New Clients?

Another criterion that you might use to select the right financial advisor is to determine whether they need new clients. They may *want* new clients—that can be a healthy sign. But if they *need* new clients, it may mean they are more likely to put their interests in front of yours.

Another component you should consider is whether or not the financial advisor is interviewing or vetting you in any way. At my firm, we have a two-step process to interview the prospective client and family. First, we conduct an exploratory call, which usually takes up to an hour, during which we ask a series of very pointed questions. The main goal is to determine whether we can have a positive impact on this family over many decades, as we are working on the assumption that we will be leading and advising them, their children, and possibly even their grandchildren.

The second step after the exploratory call, and only if we have concluded that they meet our criteria, is to give them the high-net-worth personality test. We are assessing to see what their proclivity and approach to their wealth truly is. For example, if a person scores high as a Gambler or even an Accumulator, that implies that we may not be able to impact them, because their approach to wealth is simply to grow more and to take risks with their existing wealth. This is not a judgment. It is simply in opposition to our firm's philosophy; family, community, and charity are key drivers of our work.

Our firm's values are FACE, which stands for family, authenticity, creativity, and empowerment. We exist to create a service and experience clients cannot obtain elsewhere. We do this first by treating them as extended **family**, leading and advising them as if their problems and concerns were our own. In fact, we are known for taking on and attacking their problems and concerns as if they were ours. We also treat each other at the firm as an extended family, which creates an environment in which integrity, trust, honesty, and merit can thrive.

The "A" stands for **authenticity**, to always act with integrity and be open and genuine in all of our dealings. We will not pretend to be anything we are not. This includes being honest about capabilities that we do not possess.

The "C" stands for **creativity**, as we strive to be visionary and innovative in providing an experience that can't be felt anywhere else.

The "E" stands for **empowerment**, which is a strong part of what wealthy families need and desire from their advisors. I have mentioned before that advice informs but leadership transforms. So, when we give clients all the tools needed to empower them to make wise decisions, we have fulfilled our values.

Only after we have concluded that we can affect a family positively over many generations and authentically work with them do we engage them in our Wealth Management Consultative Process.

Fees: What Are You Actually Paying?

Often, the costs and fees are not as easy to decipher as you might think. They can come in multiple forms. For example, if the advisor or wealth manager receives a commission or kickback from a brokerage firm, insurance company, or mutual fund company, this may not be disclosed, but it is embedded in the cost of the product.
The others are typically one of three types:

1. **A retainer fee** (e.g., $2,000 per month) or a singular project fee (e.g., $20,000 for a one-time plan)
2. **An hourly fee** for advice and analysis given, which can be on a project basis or ongoing
3. **A portfolio fee**, measured as a percentage of the account managed—we have found this to be highly effective at the virtual family office level because it aligns the growth of the family's liquid wealth to the success of the wealth advisor or virtual family office owner. Thus, it creates a compensation system that gives incentives for the virtual family office to take a long-term view. We are advising, leading, and defending the family.

DO NOT BE THE FOOL

Are you already working with a financial advisor, and if so, what are you paying? Does your advisor review your tax returns annually and meet with your CPA, your lawyer, and your insurance agent? Do they help coordinate services such as concierge, medical, and travel? Do they offer life transition counseling for your retirement or business exit? Do they have a process for learning your high-net-worth personality? Which of the nine personality types are you? Do they have a formal team of vetted experts in these areas to serve you or plug in regularly with your existing team? Do they offer tax planning, which goes well above and beyond tax preparation? Do they conduct insurance audits of your property, casualty, and business insurance to protect you, reduce costs, and consolidate billing? Do they have a clearly spelled out consultative process and stress test system for your wealth management, in order to optimize your life's existing strategies and future strategies?

A well-run virtual family office will provide all of these services—for the same cost you are already paying your existing wealth manager or financial advisor.

CHAPTER 9

GET OFF YOUR ASSETS

My challenge is how to get you off your *assets* and actually act in your own best interest to improve your life. While part of the answer is clearly within the wealth management industry itself, I truly believe that there is a better way to optimize your life, and that falls at the feet of wealthy families themselves. *Morgan Stanley is not the problem; you're the problem.* If you are complacent with the status quo, you won't act.

Successful business owners, entrepreneurs, and wealthy families often do not know how much they do not know. The good news is, they are often willing to seek greater expertise and guidance. However, we find they're understandably overwhelmed by the number of financial and life decisions that they must make.

As my firm's data has demonstrated, ultra-affluent clients are tired of being taken advantage of by the wealth management and financial advice industry. However, without the proper guidance, these families will continue to overpay for services they do not receive and be taken advantage of. After all their decades of hard work, risk-taking, and looking out for others, they deserve to be self-sufficient, live life on their own terms, and experience the dreams that they've been putting off for years.

You should be able to do more with your money than you ever thought possible. After all, you are a person of merit. I believe you deserve a team that will help you squeeze the maximum out of life and out of your business, while protecting what is most important to you.

I am reminded of a family who was debating retaining our services. A commission-based advisor had been advising them for decades. They knew deep down that they needed to get over their fear and follow through with the solutions we uncovered in their gap analysis and wealth stress test. It became evident that they were hurting each other—spouses, their children, and grandchildren.

They were passionate about two favorite causes, a local charity and their church. However, there was over $200,000 of waste and leakage annually from their portfolio due to their lack of good planning. The business was paying for insurance and no longer needed it. The lack of a tax plan was costing them dearly. Simple changes to their portfolio and planning would give back six figures a year to their bottom line, which could then be given in some form of charitable gift to the church and charity and contributed to a 529 plan for their grandchildren's college.

STAY OPEN TO RECEIVING

Someone you love will pay for your inertia, I promise. It occurs to me that the serious cases of inertia we witness in prospective clients and their failure to act in their own best interests and the interests of their family, employees, and loved ones may, in fact, be because they are not honoring an important principle. The Law of Receptivity, referred to in the book *The Go-Giver*, seems relevant here. It's pretty simple: let other people do nice things for you.

Over the years, I have noticed this dynamic in myself as well as many clients and prospective clients. In order to give, we must truly and deeply be open to receiving. I'm guilty of not honoring the law of receptivity and accepting dramatically less than I have earned or deserved. In my professional life, since discovering the fiduciary way of focusing on the clients and the team, I have gone above and beyond to create an experience and a service that our clients simply cannot obtain elsewhere. However, personally and professionally, I've also accepted cheating partners who were along for the free ride—partners who manipulated me and outright took advantage of my good nature.

People with a sense of humility, who are quite frankly the ones we prefer to work with, often underestimate their own value and importance. My conclusion is that deep inside, they may not genuinely believe that they deserve better than they are currently getting, particularly from their advisory team.

I cannot emphasize enough that taking action is much better for you, your family, the country, and the planet. Unaddressed inertia denies people of their future: your family, your grandchildren, charities, the country. They miss out on the benefits of having more efficient charitable solutions, more generational stability, more love, and less-entitled heirs.

VICTORY DECLARED!

The beauty of this work is when victory occurs. When individuals or families of merit who have worked all or most of their lives honestly and diligently—taking care of others, employing others, paying the highest taxes that fund our safety net in this country—when these people have victories, it is deeply fulfilling.

What does victory look like? It looks like the story of the grandmother who lost her legs being able to rebound and live a new life with her family still intact.* It looks like a business owner netting 30 percent more for their business than they had negotiated for themselves.* It looks like a business founder who knows exactly how much they need to net from their sale (after deal costs and taxes) to live their optimal financial life.* It looks like setting up a solid plan to amplify their charitable intent and give more to their beloved causes than they had ever dreamed possible.*

It is even more fulfilling when clients allow my team to lead them and advise them on those victories—and there are many. I'm reminded of one scenario when a wealthy woman came to us because her husband, a business owner, was cheating on her with one of his business associates*. In the beginning, when she was going through our process, she could not stop crying and was scared to death of what her future might hold, particularly because she was nearing sixty and facing the thought of beginning life anew. By implementing the wealth stress test process in conjunction with pulling in the top business and divorce attorneys in town, we helped achieve a huge victory for this woman.

We did not automatically accept the valuation of the husband's business that he had provided. We brought in counselors as needed. And over the next several years, not only did we negotiate a much better wealth settlement, we also helped her envision new paths that her life could hold, given her financial status. Today, we struggle to get her involved in ongoing strategy sessions because she is too busy traveling the world. I can't even keep track of how many countries she's visited.

Another victory is the case of a hotel mogul who built her business up over five decades and had partnered with two buyers on two separate occasions, only to be taken advantage of and have each of these people, several years apart, steal business and clients.* She retained us when she had found what she thought was the third viable buyer. We structured a tougher exit strategy that would protect her from being taken advantage of a third time. She was able to make compensation arrangements to keep her current employees happy, while also finding and vetting a new buyer to sell and hand off the business in a smooth succession plan. This was done in coordination with the tax planner, the legal team, and the wealth experts who understood every detail of her complex situation. Today, in the third year of the transition, she is beginning to truly envision new paths and the next chapter of her life. She is no longer working in the business and recently was able to take an extended trip overseas with her daughter and a friend. When we conduct ongoing strategy sessions, I can feel peace, calmness, and optimism in her.

FINDING PURPOSE AND FULFILLMENT

My own journey was full of potholes, but each obstacle helped me develop the skills and resilience to achieve greater success. I went from a lost, troubled youth to an experienced, respected wealth advisor, driven to provide genuine value to my clients rather than just chasing commissions.

Along the way, I learned the importance of surrounding myself with the right people. My partnership with a more financially savvy colleague proved invaluable, as did the loyalty of my long-time office manager, Trudy, who has been with me for over twenty-five years.

Additionally, I discovered the power of mergers and acquisitions, using them not just to grow the business but also to facilitate smooth transitions and succession planning. Navigating the emotional aspects of buying out a partner or selling off a portion of the firm has been a valuable lesson in managing change.

Today, I take great pride in the firm I've built and the positive impact I'm able to have on my clients' lives. The journey has been anything but linear, but

each setback and challenge has only strengthened
my resolve and deepened my sense of purpose. I'm
grateful for the opportunity to help others achieve
their financial goals, as I continue growing and evolv-
ing as a leader in the industry. If your goals align
with my expertise, I hope to have the opportunity to
help you too.

CONCLUSION

I would like to challenge you to fully clarify your vision for the future. I suspect you have spent more time planning an important vacation than you have on putting together your virtual family office or wealth team and vetting the best and the brightest. Would you have serious surgery without knowing that there is a tried, true, and tested process and that you have the best-in-class professional to do the surgery? Would you run your first marathon without a thoughtful, detailed training plan?

I am absolutely astonished by how many successful families do not prioritize wealth management. What is your three-year plan? What is your ultimate vision and dream? I recently began working on my twenty-five-year plan at the age of fifty-nine. I strongly encourage you to take the time to write it down.

Bob Proctor is famous for his life-changing advice "Thoughts become things." Approximately twenty-five years ago, I saw elegant pictures of a beautiful mansion with a man standing inside his home on a second-floor balcony, looking out of the two-story den windows. It struck me as being beautiful, spacious, and elegant. Flash forward two decades: my beloved wife, Sonya, and I bought our first home together. It had just such a two-story window with a balcony.

Ten years later, we bought a second home in Tampa, Florida. And wouldn't you know it? It had a beautiful two-story living room window and an indoor balcony from which you could view the lake and pool in the rear. Today, we own a seven-thousand-square-foot home with another gorgeous two-story living room window, with a view over the pool and the palm trees. A small dream stuck with me and is now a normal part of my life.

ENJOY YOUR WEALTH—YOU'VE EARNED IT

If you feel you may need a virtual family office or multifamily office, if you simply feel dissatisfied with your wealth advisory team, or if they are taking advantage of you, I encourage you to schedule an exploratory call with me. It is an opportunity for you to ask deep questions of an expert in this field, to see if Questmont can help you. In turn, we will ask you probing, thoughtful questions to determine if you are a good fit for our virtual family office. And if not, we promise to point you in the right direction.

Visit
QuestmontVFO.com
to book an exploratory call with me.

ACKNOWLEDGMENTS

I wish to acknowledge Sonya, my bestie, wife, business partner, and badass advanced planning leader.

My sister, Tina, has been my ever-present fan, even when I wasn't a fan of myself.

Thank you to my unique parents, who launched me, and to my rock-solid son, Ian.

And who could forget an amazing girl named Trudy who joined the firm in 1994 and has been with us ever since.

ABOUT THE AUTHOR
(AS IF YOU REALLY CARE!)

ACT I: BIRTH TO AGE 14

Small town Pennsylvania boy. Good guy, student, athlete, artist, son, and brother.

ACT II: AGES 15 TO 23

Uprooted abruptly to SoCal. Frightened, lost, and generally making "bad life decisions."

ACT III: AGES 24 TO 28

Righting the ship. Despite no college education, luckily landed a job selling insurance and investments for a national firm.

ACT IV: AGES 29 TO 33

Divorced, became Big Brother to a great inner-city boy, and began to distrust the industry I was in. Launched my own firm!

ACT V: AGES 34 TO 49

Slow grind to becoming an entrepreneur and building the right team. Finally married the perfect partner and adopted Ian. The VFO concept was born. Parted ways with my original partner, who didn't share my vision. My wife, Sonya, took his place, and the firm launched.

ACT VI: AGES 50 TO 60

My inner creative and entrepreneur began to emerge. Acquired another firm and merged in two more. Launched a branch in Tampa. Felt compelled to write this book after thirty-five years of watching successful business owners go uneducated, unprepared, and frequently taken advantage of by the "Circle of Vultures."